Conversations about Time Travel and Teleporters

JASON WERBELOFF
HELEN SARAH ROBERTSON
MARK OPPENHEIMER

OBSIDIAN WORLDS PUBLISHING

Conversations about Time Travel and Teleporters
Copyright: Jason Keith Werbeloff, Mark Oppenheimer, Helen Sarah Robertson
Editor: Yolande Coetser
Publisher: Obsidian Worlds Publishing, Johannesburg, South Africa
Published: 1 December 2021

All rights reserved. This book or any portion thereof may not be reproduced or used in any manner whatsoever without the express written permission of the publisher except for the use of brief quotations in a book review.

Contents

Foreword i

The Possibility of Time Travel 1

Star Trek, Teleporters and Personal Identity 29

Should You Have Children? 67

Torture, Heating Ducts, and Libertarianism 77

Superheroes and Vegetarians 88

Love, Lobsters, and Polyamory 98

Can You Rape a Hologram? 108

AI Orgasms, the Apocalypse, and Your Immortal Soul 116

Marriage and the Impossibility of Choice 125

The Taste of Gore 134

About the Authors 143

Foreword

I first became fascinated with philosophical questions related to time travel after seeing them represented in film. This was before I even knew what philosophy was. I'm not alone. Many people who grew up on series such as the *Planet of the Apes*, *Back to the Future*, *Harry Potter*, and the like will have been similarly enthralled by the paradoxes of time travel. What I wish I had, then, was an accessible, yet sustained, discussion of the philosophical issues that interested me. Without that, I was doomed to remain in Plato's Cave until I could take philosophy courses at university.

Time Travelers and Teleporters offers exactly what I needed and more. It begins with an amusing story that illustrates the Grandfather Paradox, which is used to set-up the insightful discussion between Jason Werbeloff, Helen Robertson, and Mark Oppenheimer. In a mere 28 pages, they provide an impressively in-depth analysis of core issues surrounding backwards time travel, while drawing the reader in through the dialectic format. This format instantly made me feel as if I were part of the conversation.

Some models of backwards time travel (e.g. the branching model) raise questions about personal identity. If I enter a parallel universe whenever I "travel back in time," am I interacting with my friends and family or are they really different people who are just qualitatively identical to my friends and family? What makes one persist through time and space?

These questions serve as the perfect segue into the next chapter on personal identity. Chapter two opens with a discussion of a *Star Trek* episode seemingly inspired by the work of Derek Parfit. Two individual beings (Tuvok and Neelix) are inadvertently fused into one being with one perspective (Tuvix). Captain Janeway can reverse the process, bringing Tuvok and Neelix back into existence, but will have to "kill" Tuvix, against his will, to do so. What should she do?

These chapters alone are worth the cover price, but there is a lot more philosophy packed into this short book. Time travel and personal identity serve as the focal point of the text, reemerging in later chapters. They also serve as a jumping-off point for exploring a variety of other philosophical issues ranging from moral sainthood to what the film *The Lobster* tells us about the nature of love.

Chapter three opens with the story of *Children of Men* and asks why having children is supposedly necessary to give life meaning. Jason Werbeloff canvases different answers to this question, showing that each of them come up short. This raises the question of whether there is *any* reason for humanity to survive. Typical anti-natalists think not and often argue for their position by appealing to the claim that so many humans (and non-human animals) have lives that contain more bad than good. It's tempting to brush these anti-natalist concerns aside, at least if you reasonably believe that you can give a child a life that contains more good than bad. Werbeloff argues, however, that if you're in this position, you should adopt an already existing suffering child and give them a good life rather than creating a new child altogether.

Chapter four reviews the wholly unique masterpiece *Brazil* and its uncompromising case for political anarchism. In the film, the state is portrayed as "a polymorphous monstrosity, with tentacles that disrupt every aspect of private life" (p. 79). Still, anarchism might be an overcorrection from totalitarianism. Could libertarianism offer a safe landing pad between these two extremes? Werbeloff argues that it cannot, nor can Mill's famous *Harm Principle*. The reader is left with a more radical conclusion, namely, that politics is nonsense since the very question of how the state should act towards its citizens is confused.

Chapter five covers two issues that are close to my heart, vegetarianism and *not* being a moral saint. Though I've never fallen short of my commitment to vegetarianism, I do fall short of moral sainthood on a daily basis. This chapter draws upon the film *Captain America: Civil War* to motivate Susan Wolf's argument against always aiming to be morally best. If Wolf is right, I can rest somewhat easier about my consistent failure at achieving moral sainthood.

Chapter six opens with a detailed synopsis of one of my all-time favorite films, *The Lobster*, in order to illustrate two different views about the nature of love (and the detrimental problems with each). In doing so, the reader is introduced to the Gellner Paradox. If we ought to love someone because they have some relevant lovable properties, then it seems that we ought to love everyone who has the same relevant properties. But, the nature of (romantic) loving relationships are often presumed to be exclusive. So, either love is impossible if this view is correct or, perhaps, people should embrace polyamory.

Questions about personal identity and ethics arise again in chapter seven. In another *Star Trek* episode, Tuvok will literally die if he doesn't copulate with another Vulcan. Since he cannot reach his wife in time, the holodeck is used to create a perfect AI replica of her, with whom Tuvok fornicates. Assuming the AI is conscious (and in this fiction, it seems to be), it falsely believes that it *is* Tuvok's wife. Consequently, it cannot consent to mate with Tuvok even if it believes it is consenting. Tuvok's actions, argues Werbeloff, are thus wrong.

Perhaps viewers had misleading intuitions in that *Star*

Trek episode because they assume AIs cannot, in fact, be conscious. Chapter eight explores whether it's possible for an immaterial AI to experience emotions through the modern cinematic classic *Her*. Drawing from Thomas Nagel's seminal *What is it Like to be a Bat?*, Werbeloff argues that it is not.

Philosophy has an undeserved reputation for being impractical. This reputation is combated in chapter nine, where the question of whether anyone should marry is taken up. The plot of the film *Mr. Nobody* is used to raise issues about promises and personal identity. Over the course of many years we completely change, both in terms of the atoms that compose our body and in terms of our character traits. Marriage typically requires making a promise that extends over the course of many years, a promise that, it's argued, may be impossible to make since it extends beyond the time our (personal) identity can be maintained.

The final chapter highlights the, perhaps problematic, film *Hardcore Henry* as an example of tasteless gore. Why do people enjoy gory films? When is depicting gore morally objectionable? After considering and rebutting various proposals, these questions are left unanswered. Depicting gore is sometimes objectionable and sometimes unobjectionable. Interestingly, more precise answers remain elusive. Like the early Platonic dialogues, this last chapter is deliberately aporetic, and appropriately so. It serves as a helpful reminder that philosophy is an ongoing discussion, where much progress has been made, and yet, there remains much progress to make.

This little book packs quite a punch. It covers a wide array of philosophical issues in a way that is accessible to any intelligent reader. This allows each chapter to engage its readers about core philosophical issues without talking down to them. It will be a delight to read for anyone interested in philosophy, science fiction, or film. If you're one of these people, you're in for a treat. If you're not, you're missing out.

TRAVIS TIMMERMAN

November 2021

The Possibility of Time Travel

Helen Robertson

Let us suppose that Mark's grandfather, Mel, and Mark himself both have a great love for fine malt whisky. From time to time Mark has Mel over for a whisky evening and they taste whisky together and discuss the finer points of their shared hobby. But then suppose, Mark realises that Mel has designs on his whisky collection. Mark in fact starts to feel quite threatened and decides that something needs to be done to protect his collection. In fact, he decides extreme measures are needed and so gets himself a firearm and goes for some shooting lessons. He becomes quite a good shot.

Mark knows Mel's movements and where he lives. So, he lurks in the bushes outside and waits for Mel to arrive home. He has got a clear view and when Mel arrives home, Mark takes his shot and hits and kills Mel. This is the first case.

In the second case, Jason comes along to Mark and tells him that he used his science fiction novels as a blueprint to build a time machine and that it is in the spare room of his flat. He tells Mark that he's welcome to use it any time he likes.

Mark thinks this provides a way of nipping the whisky thief issue in the bud. He thinks that if he can travel back in time, he can kill Mel long before he even develops an interest in whisky. It offers him a means to go back and stop this threat at source. So, he climbs into the time machine, dials in the relevant dates and travels back to Mel's teenage years. He lands in Johannesburg, with his firearm, in 1935. But when he lands, he's got a bit of time to spare and as he knows the new City Library is due to be formally opened the next day, he decides to go and have a look. After that he intends intercepting the young Mel and sorting the situation out. While he's inspecting the new library building, he steps into some wet concrete and leaves his footprints. These become permanent fixtures and today it is still possible to go and look at Mark's footprints in the concrete outside the Johannesburg City Library.

So, Mark is back in 1935 in Johannesburg and once again he is lurking in the bushes waiting for Mel. He's still trained to use his firearm and, when Mel arrives, he has a clear shot. It seems exactly like the same situation that the Mark of 2020 was in immediately before he shot and killed the older Mel. Yet we know that Mel has not yet married his future wife and sired Mark's father who has not yet in turn sired Mark. It simply cannot be that Mark can shoot Mel. There isn't any possible world in which Mark is able to shoot Mel.

The paradox – the Grandfather paradox – is essentially the contrast between the two cases. On the one hand, there's Mark in 2020, trained up and we know he can shoot Mel the moment he has a clear shot. On the other, there's Mark in 1935, with the same skills but unable to shoot Mel. It's not clear why. What we really want is some sort of account of why in the 1935 case,

Mark is unable to kill Mel, even though the cases seem the same in terms of Mark's capacities, the physical set-up, and the opportunity.

MARK OPPENHEIMER

One of the ways of solving the paradox is that I can shoot at Mel but when I do so the bullet misses – so we don't have the sort of impossibility problem of Mel never having kids and me never being born and therefore never being able to shoot him. Alternatively, perhaps we have a parallel universe that gets created and really what I've done is not kill Mel but kill Mel Two in this other parallel universe. That allows me to still be born because original Mel survives, and it's only parallel Mel that gets killed. But then, I wonder, is this still a genuine case of time travel? Part of why we find the idea of time travel so alluring is this idea of being able to fix our pasts.

People are inclined to look back on the mistakes they perceive themselves to have made. A guy might think he married the wrong woman. If only he could go back in time and never meet her, then he wouldn't be in this miserable marriage with these three screaming children. The urge may be more noble. You may want to stop John F. Kennedy being assassinated or Idi Amin coming to power. In all cases it's a matter of undoing what has happened. What I'm asking is if, in the parallel universe case, we're not just sidestepping the problem. Because all we're doing is creating a whole new parallel set of problems?

HELEN ROBERTSON

I think that's right. It's a commonly accepted view in the Philosophy of Time that there are two sorts of questions here. On the one hand, there's the question of changing the past. It's generally thought that to change the past is not a possibility. So, if we think that time travel of some sort is possible, it's not going to be of the sort that involves changing the past. Then there's the other question which is that of parallel universes or time-splitting. There again, it's not a genuine case of time travel or at least not the sort that we're interested in. Paradigm cases of genuine time travel are cases in which we do travel significantly forward to the future or back to the past, but in which the timeline on which we are located is consistent. We have to travel within the history of this world and the timeline of this world. If you have time-splitting or end up doing something that didn't occur in our actual history, those are generally not thought to be genuine cases of time travel.

JASON WERBELOFF

Yes, the parallel worlds solution isn't really satisfying. Because, as we agree, we want to go back and affect *our* history – not some other parallel history. We want to affect *our* past so that we can affect *our* present.

But there's another version of time travel, which I encountered in a collection of short stories by Ted Chiang. In *Exhalation*, the narrator buys into the idea of fatalism. This is no more satisfying than Mark's time splitting. In some ways it's even more infuriating. Chiang asks us to imagine walking into a shop one day in Baghdad. You walk in and there is a mirror on the wall. Except it's not an ordinary mirror. If you look carefully, what you see is not a reflection of yourself but of the store as it was in the past. The 'mirror' is actually a time portal. You ask the store owner how far the portal goes backwards and he tells you that it depends on how he sets it. This particular setting goes back three years. So, you say oh, that's amazing. There are all sorts of things I would like to do. I'd like to go back three years and tell my previous self not to get hit by that car on that particular day, or not to marry that awful woman, or tell my previous self what the lottery numbers were going to be that day.

The store owner sighs, and let's you through. "You can try," he says. "You wouldn't be the first."

So you go to the past with plans to change your life. But try as you might to change the past, you can't. No matter what you tell your past self, he still gets hit by that car – or perhaps he gets hit by the car running away from the terrifying visage of his future self! You try to convince your prior self that you shouldn't marry that woman, but your previous self is rebellious and marries her *because* you told him not to.

In other words, in Chiang's writing, time travel generates a fatalistic circularity. You causally influence the past to become what you remember the past to be. But you can't change it.

HELEN ROBERTSON

That sounds like a great story. It certainly picks up on a quite important distinction between influencing the past and actually changing the past. What we're interested in is the possibility of changing the past. So, in a person's own life a series of events has happened. Some of them are mistakes. What we're interested in, in the case of time travel, is going back to these events and changing them or ensuring that the mistakes weren't made. But it's generally accepted that it's not possible to change the past because this involves some sort of logical contradiction. So, we're essentially making a claim that, setting aside parallel universes or pushing time or strange things like that, assumes a kind of linear time. We are saying that this world is made up of a series of events that take place in time. The course of history includes events A, B, and C. We're suggesting that it's not open to us to make it the case that history doesn't include A, B and C. These events are already part of the setup. Insofar as we may want to be able to go back in time and change the past, this is bad news.

This is the point argued by people like Paul Horwich. Insofar as time travel is tempting in this form, it's bad news for all of us, right? But there is another distinction which is important. Horwich, who wrote in the 1970s, addresses the distinction between influencing the past and changing the past. Because you can't change something that has already taken place, it doesn't mean that you couldn't initially have had some causal role in that event.

The idea is that (assuming time travel is possible) it is incorrect to suppose that somebody could go back and causally influence the past. It cannot be that history first looked like this and then, after a causal intervention, it looked different. History always contained the intervention. It was always the case that Mark went back and left a footprint in the setting concrete in front of the library. He isn't able to go back and not leave the footprint. So, potentially, there are cases in which you can go back and have a causal influence of some sort.

JASON WERBELOFF

This is where my brain struggles. In movies and a lot of fiction about time travel, there are these causal loops. There's a movie where a man goes back in time and meets a young woman who turns out to be his mother. But he doesn't know this, so he has a relationship with her and begets himself, who then goes back in time and has a relationship with his mother and begets himself and so on in a never-ending loop. But is that loop logically possible? If it is then why am I so uncomfortable thinking about it (beyond the fact that it involves incest)? I'm struggling to formulate the precise problem ...

HELEN ROBERTSON

This is a sort of loop. It contrasts very nicely with the sort of loop that we get in the case of the grandfather paradox. In the case of the grandfather paradox, the causal loop has a link that requires a prior link. But that prior link 'destroys' the subsequent link. So, in the case of the grandfather paradox, it seems like we have an inconsistent causal loop, which we do genuinely think is a problem. Whereas in the case you've described – where you go back and you meet your lovely young mother – again, we certainly have a causal loop. But it doesn't seem inconsistent in the way the grandfather paradox loop is. In this case, we have a consistent causal loop in the sense that each cause is giving rise to some effect, and not eliminating the subsequent effects.

You're asking whether such a causal loop is problematic? We can ask this in various ways. We can ask whether it is logically, metaphysically, or physically possible or impossible.

On the question of logical possibility and impossibility,

I think it is impossible only if you take on fairly strong assumptions about some things having a sufficient reason that potentially you're going to arrive at some sort of logical contradiction. If we consider views of cause and effect that were held in early modern times – where the idea was that everything that happens must have a sufficient reason – it seems that this causal loop (even though it's consistent) does not in itself have a sufficient reason. Every link in the causal loop is just the reason for every prior link. If you have strong commitments like this, then this might seem problematic. But I don't think too many people have such strong commitments.

The physical possibility or impossibility question falls within the theory of general relativity. I'm certainly no physicist, but greatly simplified, the claim is that there is a consistent notion of an essentially closed causal loop, a closed time-like curve (or CTC). The idea is that a material particle could have, what translates as its path in time within general relativity, a path that was closed. So, at least within certain physical theories which we haven't yet transcended, it's consistent to have some version of a closed causal series.

Mark Oppenheimer

So, the first moral of the story is, you can fuck your mother, but you can't kill your grandfather. The reason why Jason can't remember the name of the movie is because it sounds like an X-rated version of Back to the Future, where Marty McFly actually winds up having sex with his mother, instead of trying desperately to get his parents to be together.

Back to the Future is a paradigmatic time travel movie where something odd is going on. Marty McFly and Doc go back in time to 1955 where Marty meets his mother – who thinks that his name is Calvin Klein because that's what is sewn into his underwear – and she becomes besotted with him. At some point he realises that this is his mother and that if he doesn't ensure that she meets his father at this big dance, he will cease to exist. There are moments in the movie when that starts to happen. He becomes transparent. There is the sense that if he doesn't act quickly, he will cease to exist and fade away. He is ultimately successful and is able to ensure that his parents meet each other and fall in love. He also does a few other things which change reality. The bad guy in the movie, Biff, starts in 1985, at the beginning of the movie, as wealthy and successful but still an unpleasant bully. But when Marty gets back to his 'correct' time (1985) he finds Biff is a loser who is washing his dad's car instead of the other way around. And Marty's dad has become a successful writer. There's a sort of time tinkering that has gone on but also some sort of updating of the possibility of time. Is this account of time travel consistent with the philosophical models? Or is it just pure fiction?

HELEN ROBERTSON

At least part of what you've described in Back to the Future case – Marty going back and setting it up such that his parents should meet – doesn't strike me as problematic. It might raise Jason's concern about closed causal loops, but if we're thinking only about the influencing the past business, then there is nothing about it which is inconsistent.

It is similar to what happens to Harry Potter in The Prisoner of Azkaban. Harry and Hermoine are hiding out by Hagrid's hut and there is a point where Hermoine throws a stone at the hut. That happens earlier in the plot. But Harry, who's inside the hut, experiences it quite a bit later in the narrative. Harry and Hermione have always had an effect on something that happens to their future selves. By currently-accepted models, these sorts of cases are fine. They just count as a case of having a causal effect on the past, but do not imply the claim that the past is some way different to the way we know it is.

So, these sorts of cases, like Harry experiencing the thrown stone later or Marty getting his parents to meet up, in at least that respect they don't fare too badly, in philosophical terms.

Mark Oppenheimer

The implication is that there must always have been a Calvin Klein, who got the parents to meet, and it just happened to be that it was their son. Think about space and time. A novel proceeds in a chronological way. But actually, it exists in one physical form in one time. It's a physical object made of paper bound between covers. But when we're reading it, we have this illusion of time changing. In the novel, there may be a series of events that occur, and it is only when we get to page 1 000 that we find out one of the characters is a time traveler who has determined the set of events. So that the levels of causation might not be in the direction we expected.

But they are fixed, in that the novel is the way it is written. And there is no other way that it could be. It just happens that the cause emanates from the future rather than the past.

HELEN ROBERTSON

This raises two important points. One is the case of influencing the past, simply because the past has always been as it is. In the case of the novel, it has always been the case that the character did certain things. We can't go back and rewrite the pages of the novel. The claim is that just because the past always was this way – including someone who has gone back in time and causally affected the past – there's no reason to suppose they weren't able to do otherwise.

The other point is the block universe account, which we get to because there are other problems posed for the possibility of time travel depending on what view we have of time itself.

To get back to the first question of it not entailing change: If we suppose that someone's gone back in the past – Mark has left a shoe print in the concrete, Marty McFly has ensured that his parents met – the philosophical account supposes that we need to think of that as having always been the case. History was always like that. But the claim doesn't entail that it couldn't have been otherwise. It doesn't raise problems for views of freedom (depending on what views of freedom we hold). The way to see this is to think of cases of the future.

Tomorrow, we're all going to wake up and wonder what we are going to do with the day. Mark has already done Mel in so he's got to think of something new to do. Suppose Mark and Jason have a chat and decide who the next guest on Brain in a Vat is going to be. They ask this person to join them and their chosen guest agrees. So, it will be the case that it is true that Mark and Jason have this person on their show. Given that this is true in the future, it's not possible to make it false. It doesn't mean that they didn't freely choose or couldn't have done otherwise. Once Mark and Jason had decided and acted, the future then contained this person being your next guest. It is the same with the past.

When Mark travels back to 1935 Johannesburg and is trying to decide whether to take the day off and go to the library opening or just shoot Mel or do some more firearm training to improve his chances of success, the claim is that there is genuine choice involved. Mark can choose to do otherwise, and things could go wrong, or not. But once he has decided and acted, then history is fixed. It's important to distinguish between the idea of history being fixed only once all of this has happened from the idea of history being fixed in advance. The latter is a fatalistic view where regardless of what anyone may want or decide, things will always turn out a certain way.

JASON WERBELOFF

Now I'm confused. Let's say Mark goes back to 1935. He walks past the library where they're setting the concrete in the sidewalk. He steps into the concrete, leaving his footprints. Now, just before Mark travelled back in time, he was in 2020. It that year there just happens to be these footprints in the sidewalk right. They've been there ever since Mark can remember and just happen to match the shoes Mark has in 2020. Mark then goes back in time to 1935 when there's no footprint yet. Surely it is now determined that Mark must then step in that setting concrete, otherwise it would contradict the experiences that he then has later in his life – there will not be a footprint in 2020 for him to remember seeing in that concrete. So, while you could say that he could have done otherwise, as soon as he travels back in time, freedom appears to vanish.

HELEN ROBERTSON

There's an argument in the literature which distinguishes between the two cases. The distinction turns on what that footprint is dependent on. So, we want to say, yes, in the future, he's seen this footprint, he's got the memory of the footprint and now he goes back in time. When he does so, it seems to him that he that he can't do other than step into the concrete. So, his actions in 1935 are determined. But the claim against this is that we still get a consistent picture if Mark, in 1935, had made a decision to leave his footprint in the concrete. He then goes on to see it many years later and has this memory.

JASON WERBELOFF

This is where I start to get tripped up by the issue of freedom. There are two different accounts of freedom: compatibilism and incompatibilism. The compatibilist view is that it is possible for you to be free *and* for all of your decisions in the world to be determined. What does 'determined' mean in this context? It means that given certain conditions at a certain time, the world would have to be a certain way at a later time. Given that you make this decision, something *will* happen in the future and, given what happened in the past, you *are* going to make this decision. By contrast, incompatibilists argue that that's not freedom and you can't be considered free under those conditions. They insist that what freedom requires is indeterminism. It must be the case that given conditions at a previous time, you could make different choices at this time. So, is there freedom just in the compatibilist sense? Have you assumed determinism?

HELEN ROBERTSON

My suspicion is that the account of time travel I've given here will sit quite happily with the compatibilist account. I'm not entirely sure that it sits happily with the incompatibilist account with its strong free will. If we say a person is free if they have the right psychological setup and are not unduly influenced by external circumstances or strange and unfortunate internal influences, then we're going to see this as a case of free will. So, given these caveats, this decision or this action counts as a free action. In the case of Mark in 1935 we can assume he has free will. Mark has really chosen to make that footprint. Even if he decided to walk this way around the building rather than that way and just happens to step in the concrete, we would still think that that counts as a free action. This account definitely sits fine with compatibilist views.

In that example, I was setting aside this question. After we introduced causal loops into the discussion, we get a situation where Mark was aware of the footprints before making them and this awareness was maybe entering into his reasons for doing it.

In the case of incompatibilism, there are problems which may be even bigger. The strong version of free will wreaks much havoc with views of cause and effect and what's going on in the physical world anyway.

Mark Oppenheimer

Let's think about it this way. Let's say that a week ago I make a choice to order in some Chinese food. I did all the weighing up, I thought about my options, and I made a free choice to order Chinese food. Today I ask myself, is it possible for Mark a week ago to not order Chinese food? It's impossible. The thing has occurred and I cannot alter that fact. But there was a time when I was free to do so (a week ago). I suppose what's tricky is to work out when was that time that you were free? Let's say I intentionally put my foot in the concrete because I want to leave a footprint. But the reason that I did so is because I have seen that footprint 70 years later. So, in 1935, there is some kind of funny, compelling force that's playing a role in my choice. While I might be free at the time, there's also some sense in which I could not do otherwise.

Helen Robertson

I think this is the concern that's getting to Jason as well. I wanted to distinguish fatalism (where you genuinely don't have other options and things are going to turn out a certain way regardless of what you do) from the sort of thing that was going on in these time travel cases. I've tried to argue that not all cases of time travel must involve fatalism. This I put in the form of the claim that it is possible for the time traveler to do otherwise in the moment. Even though history plays itself out in some way, nonetheless other possibilities are open to people at the time of their action.

I think Jason still thinks that there's a worrying difference between claiming this with regard to the future and claiming it for the time traveler going back into the past. In the case of the future I genuinely have a range of possibilities open to me. Of course, once I've chosen and acted on that choice then history is the way that it is and can't be changed. This is not incompatible with the claim that I do have options.

Jason's concern is that when it comes to traveling into the past, the same scale of opportunity for free choice does not seem to be available. There are cases, as we've seen, where what happens in the future does determine what the time traveler does in the past. The short stories by Ted Chiang or Mark's 1935 footprint in the concrete seem to involve some sort of compulsion or determinism running from the future to shape or constrain the time traveler's options. What we need to find to refute the fatalist viewpoint is just one case where the structure of the future does not determine past actions.

I think the footprint on concrete event is one such case. If Mark was walking around Johannesburg in 1935, there are many roads he could have chosen to go down. He could take this road or that road. Assuming he has no prior memories influencing his choice of roads, it's not clear that he wouldn't genuinely have a range of options. He could choose to walk down this street or that street. If that's the case, then we have found at least one instance where the fatalist problem doesn't arise.

Have I persuaded either of you?

Mark Oppenheimer

It seems to me that what you've done is set up a parallel. In the original grandfather paradox, it is a logical impossibility which means you cannot kill your own grandfather. There might also be a logical requirement that I have to put my shoes into the cement in 1935. But in between, there's a whole bunch of freedom and that's going to be where you have to make your case.

We've been talking about some classic sci fi and some great time travel movies but I want give a more recent example. In an episode of Rick and Morty called 'The Vat of Acid Episode'. Morty tells Rick that there's something he really wants him to invent. He wants a 'revert' button for real life. You know how if you're playing an old Nintendo game you can save your game and carry on from that point later. If you die, it's okay, you just revert back to the save game settings.

Rick is very resistant to this idea, but eventually agrees and somewhat later gives Morty the device. The first thing Morty does is ask out the prettiest girl in the school. But it goes very badly so Morty uses the 'revert' button to reset the world to one where he hadn't made such a mess. He tries again and this time he's more nonchalant and the girl responds and becomes obsessed with him. He keeps using the revert button. He tries to jump over a manhole but falls in. So, he hits the revert button, tries again and succeeds. This device helps him meet someone, fall in love and go on a trip with her. He in fact lives a whole other life but eventually hits the revert button after having a plane crash.

Rick insists that this is not time travel but something else. Now, how do we distinguish these things? Because in the story Morty is going back in time to some prior state where he hit the 'Save' button?

HELEN ROBERTSON

This is a great case. But in the end, it does seem to be time travel in some sense, the difference being that it is not a possible version. It seems to me to be a case of continually changing of the past. History contains a series of events and, in this version, you can mark a certain point as the moment you are going to rewind to. History, as we understand it, goes on. Events are taking place and time is passing in the ways that we normally think of it happening, and then suddenly all of this gets denied. Suddenly, it gets claimed that these events haven't taken place. A philosopher's concern is that this is just contradictory. It's not clear to me that we are talking any longer talking about traveling within time as we understand it.

JASON WERBELOFF

The problem is that philosophers don't like contradictions. We're saying that contradictions are impossible. And given that traveling back in time would allow you to generate a contradiction by killing your grandfather, for example, traveling back in time is impossible. That's version one. Version two is that traveling back in time is possible, so long as it does not generate a contradiction and will not influence the past in ways that will generate a paradox. I'm talking about genuine time travel, not travel to a parallel timeline. Is the consensus that time travel into the past is possible only for travelers who do not generate a contradiction?

HELEN ROBERTSON

I think the jury's out. But many philosophers do hold the view that we can formulate a version of time travel, along with an account which needs to explain what's going on in the grandfather paradox. So, we can give a relatively substantive, consistent account of what time travel would look like. According to that view time travel is possible, at least insofar as it is not logically contradictory, and it doesn't involve any of these things that generate paradoxes. The difficult thing to do is to then give an account of why these paradoxes are not going to be generated. In the 1970s, David Lewis set out to defend the possibility of time travel. He postulates an explanation of why paradoxes don't occur - why Mark is not able to kill Mel in 1935. Something intervenes! Mark slips on a banana peel or is distracted by a bird or Mel trips and the shot misses.

This seems to me to be rather problematic. It seems fine in any single case but when we try to generalise it as an explanation, we have to rely on a series of random events. In every single case, we're not able to take action because something weird happens. That doesn't make for a very convincing general account of what's going on.

Mark Oppenheimer

So, you have a series of events, which in and of themselves are perfectly ordinary, but in fact they combine to prevent me killing Mel. That seems incredibly unlikely.

HELEN ROBERTSON

Yes, precisely. The concern is that you've got to have strong correlations between what may be termed 'foiling circumstances' (circumstances that foil your killing of your grandfather) in order to avoid generating contradictions. And on the other hand, you're going to have a kind of lack of explanation of why it's not possible to kill your grandfather.

JASON WERBELOFF

We've been talking about time traveling to the past. Am I right in suggesting that none of these contradictions pop up if you travel into the future?

HELEN ROBERTSON

Yes, there are definitely far fewer contradictions that tend to come up or paradoxes that are posed about future time travel. This is due to what is commonly termed the arrow of time or the asymmetry of time. If we're thinking of the characteristics of time in contrast to space, there are many ways in which time is asymmetric while space isn't. Generally, we can carry out actions in the future direction, not in the past direction whereas in the case of space, we can carry out actions in any direction. Similarly, we only have knowledge about the past and not the future, whereas there doesn't seem to be the same sort of asymmetry in the case of space. The fact that a lot of the paradoxes arise in cases of time travel to the past has got to do with these asymmetries. This is why there's been a lot of philosophical work done on this idea that time moves from the past to the future, and that there are all these asymmetries associated with temporal locations and not spatial locations.

STAR TREK, TELEPORTERS AND PERSONAL IDENTITY

JASON WERBELOFF

In Season Two of *Star Trek Voyager*, Neelix and Tuvok are teleported down to a planet to collect plant specimens (more about the teleporter [they call it the 'transporter'] shortly). Neelix is loud. Gregarious. He's the chef, and the ship's morale officer. He's also particularly ugly.

Tuvok, on the other hand, is a Vulcan. Reserved,

logical, considered. He's the ship's ultra-serious security chief. At the spritely age of at least a century (his real age is a closely guarded secret), Tuvok might be considered the opposite personality pole of Neelix. This is what makes the events that ensue particularly interesting.

So, Tuvok and Neelix have been teleported down to an alien planet to collect plant samples. After plenty of bickering – unsurprisingly, the two don't like each other – they achieve their mission, and are teleported back to the ship. But, little do they know, the plant they just harvested has the property of muddling DNA. The result is that instead of the expected *two* individuals on the teleportation pad on the ship, when they beam them up there is only *one* person. The alien plant messed with the teleporter, and caused it to combine the two officers together, resulting in ... Tuvix.

The ship's crew panics. We need to separate Tuvix into his component persons ASAP, declares Captain Janeway. The Doctor sets to work finding a solution. But the problem is that the plant enzymes have scrambled their DNA so badly, he says there's no quick way to separate out Tuvix.

Tuvix is happy and healthy, however. He has the culinary and social skills of Neelix, and the logical and rational capacity of Tuvok. As a combination of the two, he's an extraordinary crew member, capable of more than either of Neelix or Tuvok. (He's also slightly less ugly than Neelix, which is a plus.)

Weeks pass, during which Tuvix develops relationships that neither of his progenitors had before him. He forms new bonds, develops new skills, and becomes a valued, contributing member of the crew.

And, here lies the dilemma. Eventually, the Doctor finds a way to separate out Tuvix into his component persons. Initially when Tuvix appeared on the teleporter pad, he was happy to be separated out. But now, weeks later, he's far more reluctant. He appeals to the Doctor and Captain Janeway. I'm more than the sum of my original parts, he pleads. I'm neither Neelix nor Tuvok. They're dead. I'm Tuvix – a distinct individual with my own rights. And if you separate me out, I'll die. You'll be murdering me.

Captain Janeway is faced with an awful dilemma. On the one hand, if she leaves Tuvix as he is, she's consigning Neelix and Tuvok to oblivion. Tuvok has a wife and children. They'll never see him again. And Neelix has a particularly gorgeous Ocampan girlfriend on board (why she chose Neelix is bizarre), who misses him dreadfully. She doesn't bond with Tuvix the way she'd loved Neelix.

On the other hand, if Janeway separates out Tuvix into his component persons, she's committing murder, and denying the individuality of a man who is clearly an individual. She's undermining the value of the relationships and skills that Tuvix has developed since his inception weeks earlier.

So, what should Captain Janeway do? Separate Tuvix or not?

MARK OPPENHEIMER

Let's assume for the sake of argument that we have this new being that has popped into existence in the form of Tuvix. One way we might think about that being is by comparing it to a new-born child. Two parents have combined their DNA to produce the child which has attributes of both, but is at the same time its own independent being.

Jason Werbeloff

Tuvix actually makes that comparison in the show. He says he feels like Tuvok and Neelix are his 'parents'.

Mark Oppenheimer

Now let's imagine a situation where after the child is born, the mother falls into a coma. And that's such a shock to the father that he too lapses into a coma. So the child is adopted and goes on living, making friends and leading a normal life. But then the doctors say they've made a breakthrough and they can revive both parents. The catch is that they have to kill the child to do so because they need to harvest its organs to make the antidote. So, the question is whether it is okay to kill the child to save the parents?

I think we should feel pretty uncomfortable about this suggestion. The act of killing is wrong even if the benefit is twofold (killing one to save two). If the only way that you could save or reanimate the parents is through killing, then you can't do it.

Jason Werbeloff

I wonder whether you're not using a deontological framework here? For background, there are two different kinds of ethical systems, utilitarianism on the one hand, and deontology or Kantianism on the other. On the deontological framework, you should respect human dignity. In this case, Tuvix is a person, and thus should expect to be treated as a being with full moral rights.

On the other hand, there's the utilitarian framework which says you must do what is best for society as a whole, taking everyone's interests into consideration. So, you might provide a utilitarian argument for separating Tuvix because you're saving two and killing one. Whereas the deontological argument says, you can't ever sacrifice anyone. So, is that what you're trying to get at Mark? Are you trying to give a deontological account?

Mark Oppenheimer

It's not a simple calculation for a utilitarian because it's not merely matter of saying, well, one life versus two lives. The goodness of these lives is going to play a role. As you pointed out, Tuvix is greater than the sum of his parts. They specifically make that point in the episode. He is a better cook because he possesses rationality and he makes better strategic decisions because he's aware of emotion.

The other interesting element is that he falls in love with Neelix's girlfriend, and you get the strong sense from her, that she'd like to pursue a relationship. Of course, she feels grief over the death of Neelix and thus some hesitation. But there's a line where she says, 'You know, I think we can be friends, and maybe more'. There are interesting side questions about whether she is moving in or moving on. But what really complicates things is that Tuvix isn't just a new being. He holds the memories of the prior two beings simultaneously. So, it's not clear to me on a utilitarian calculation what you ought to do, because Tuvix might actually be better than the other two. You've also got to ask if he is identical with the other two? Or is he the other two plus something new?

JASON WERBELOFF

This is the fascinating question. Is he one person? Or is he three? Is he Tuvok *and* Neelix *and* the combination? Or is he just the combination? To muddy the waters further, in the episode, Tuvix keeps portraying himself as having qualities of both his 'parents'. He has perfect memory of everything that happened to both Tuvok and Neelix. He has all their memories and feels the same way about his previous partners. Tuvok has a wife on Planet Vulcan and Neelix has his girlfriend and the new synthesis personality, Tuvix, still has feelings for both. He's a combined being. So, a utilitarian could argue, if he wanted to save Tuvix, that he is now actually equivalent in value to three lives, not just one.

But now let's ask this question: is he a continuation of Tuvok and Neelix? This is where we might refer to a great philosopher, someone whose work I admire enormously, Derek Parfit.

Parfit used a series of thought experiments to argue that identity is not one-to-one relation. In other words, it's not the case that you exist at a certain time and that there is necessarily at a later time just one of you. Also, to Parfit, there's no golden thread — i.e. it's not the case that what will exist tomorrow is 100 percent of you: Rather it will be some percentage of you.

Parfit invites us to consider the way you are now, compared to the way you were as a small child. How similar are you? The truth is that you're probably not very similar at all. You might have some of the memories of that child and of course that's important. But in many ways, you're very different. When I was five-years old, I had no knowledge of philosophy, I hadn't watched *Star Trek* yet, I hadn't written any science fiction books. I was a very different person to the person I am now. You know, all the things that have happened to me in my life hadn't happened back then.

Now compare me with Mark. Mark and I have a lot in common. We both love philosophy, we both host a podcast and YouTube series called Brain in a Vat, and we've both been part of very similar conversations at opposite ends of the table. Mark and I are much more similar than I am to my five-year-old self.

For Parfit, what this indicates, is that it is incorrect to say that I am just identical with my childhood self. It is much more accurate to say that there is some degree of continuity between my childhood self and me today. There's also a degree of continuity between Mark and me, which might even be greater. So, Parfit thinks that identity continues through various people to varying degrees, and that it shifts and changes throughout our lives. His idea is that identity is not a one-to-one but rather one-to-many, and that there's no golden thread of 100% identity. Rather identity gets split and moves around between the people that you meet and how you influence them.

For example, my grandmother influences me enormously. Yet she died eight years ago. I inherited her dishwasher, and I perceive her personality in that dishwasher. It's totally my grandmother, the way it doesn't run when it doesn't want to. Parfit would say there's a continuation of my grandmother in that dishwasher right, a certain percentage and a continuation of her in me.

So, in the Tuvok/Neelix case, they both continue into Tuvix, according to Parfit, because their memories continue.

MARK OPPENHEIMER

I like this analogy you've drawn with your relationship with your grandmother because if your grandmother didn't exist, you would not exist. If Jason died at the age of five, you wouldn't exist either. So, you owe your existence to these other beings, but they are separate from you. It is very easily to recognise the separateness between you and your grandmother. But we tend to think of you and the baby as being the same. This is a mistake, according to Parfit. It might be better to think rather of the baby Jason as an ancestor.

We think of this as a series of overlapping arcs. Our cells change every seven years so we know we are physically different over time. Bodies change and so do mental states. But we might think the five-year-old baby is pretty similar to the five-year-old baby plus a day, which is similar a day later and so on. There are these overlapping arcs. And at some point, the being we are now and the being we were in the past don't overlap anymore. But the current being would not exist were it not for this previous being. So, we've got an interesting thing going on for Tuvix who would not exist, were it not for Tuvok and Neelix. Tuvix is almost like a child of the other two and holds their memories in the way that you hold the memories of your predecessor states.

Now, what's cool about Parfit and *Star Trek*, is that Parfit had his own thought experiment, in which a big role is played by a teleporter.

JASON WERBELOFF

Before Parfit, philosophers generally thought that what makes me who I am is my *body*. So, I am the person I was yesterday because the body I had yesterday and the body I have today is the same.

Parfit asks us to imagine an experiment. You step onto a teleporter pad which scans you and rebuilds you on another pad. You're going to disappear from the first pad and reappear on the second pad. But is it YOU who walks away from the second pad? People say, yes it's me, because the person who walks off on the other side has all my memories (he remembers stepping on to the first pad). He has all my beliefs, my name, looks the same and feels the same as I do.

But Parfit observes that if this is the case, it's not me in terms of my *body*. The original body on the first pad has been mulched. It is destroyed, turned into particles of energy. Then a new body was created on the second pad. So, if we are our bodies, it can't be me who steps off on the second pad. So, if our intuition that it is still me who steps off the second pad is correct, then it cannot be our bodies which determine who we are.

What makes the second person the same me as the first, is that the second person who steps off on their pad has memories and thoughts and beliefs and personality traits of the first person. Parfit calls this your psychological profile. What counts is your psychological profile: that's what determines your identity.

Mark Oppenheimer

Parfit cashed the thought experiment out even further. He says imagine that there was a delay so that the receiving pad prints you off while the original is still on the first pad. So, both of you could coexist for a while. And then let's say that for legal reasons we can't have two Marks or two Jasons existing at the same time. We're going to now kill the first one. So, you could, after teleporting, watch the original version of you get destroyed. Would you still think this was you? In other words, at some point in time are you in two bodies? Where is the you-ness – is it in the physicality or is it in the mental states? And if it's in the mental states, can you have these clones of you that would still be you?

Jason Werbeloff

That's the thought experiment which is meant to show that identity is one-to-many. It's not one-to-one, because if we don't destroy the body on the original pad, then there are two of you walking around. Parfit would point out that you were perfectly willing to accept that it was you on Pad B previously, when Pad A destroyed the body. When Pad A doesn't destroy the body, you're not sure which one is you. Well, Parfit says, it's both. Who you are is both. So that means identity is one to many.

Mark Oppenheimer

What's interesting about the *Star Trek* episode is that it's many-to-one. It reverses things by combining two separate people who had no relationship with each other whatsoever. In fact, they're different kinds of space beings, right? One's a Vulcan and the other is a Talaxian. Now we've merged them into some kind of new being, a previously unknown space species, with the memories of these two prior beings. Is there one new being or is it all three? And what if I were to inject my memories into you before I died?

Jason Werbeloff

There's another philosopher who doesn't accept Parfit's argument that identity is one-to-many. Nozick argues that identity is always one-to-one. He says one of these people on teleporter Pad A or B is you and one of them is not. One of them is 100% you and the other is 0% you. It's simply a copy of you. Nozick relies on what he calls his 'closest continuer' account of personal identity. He's trying to avoid cases like Parfit's teleportation experiment as well as the case where you inject your memories into me.

Nozick says that what makes you who you are is that you are the closest continuer of your previous self. He argues there's a whole bunch of criteria that we consider when determining who is the closest continuer. One of them is your memories, but another one is your body. He believes the closest continuer will be the person who meets as many of those criteria as possible. He has a kind of calculus which pings out results which tell you who you are. So, if you inject some of your memories into me, you will not continue through me, according to Nozick. You are still you and I'm still me. The Mark body is the closest continuer of Mark and the Jason body is the closest continuer of Jason. He's fought against the intuitions that Parfit has that identity isn't one-to-one and doesn't involve a golden thread. In the Nozickian account would Tuvix be a continuation of the other two – or, to reframe it slightly – would the other two live on in Tuvix? No, I don't think so. But Parfit says the opposite. In his account they would live on in Tuvix.

Mark Oppenheimer

There's another interesting rebuttal of Nozick, again sourced from science fiction. There's a movie called The Butterfly Effect which came out about 20 years ago. There's a guy who time travels. When he returns, he carries the memories from the parallel worlds that he's been in. Once he's done this four times, he's sitting with four distinct memories of his parallel lives, all of which are him in a physical continuity sense. And it ultimately drives him mad, having to hold these parallel states from these different worlds. So, what's going on there? It seems to be one being, different memories. Is he four people or is he one person? On the Parfitian account, he is one continuous being derived from multiple sources. They all they all continue in him.

Jason Werbeloff

But it depends on whether the existence of each of those people ended in their respective dimensions. Or did they continue, in which case your Butterfly Effect guy has simply shifted back into his own dimension with their memories.

Mark Oppenheimer

You could have a quantum leap where someone inhabits one psyche but jumps between various physical bodies. So, there's no death, just a kind of movement between bodies.

Or we could imagine that the person dies in Parallel World A but is re-born in Parallel World B with all the memories of their previous life. They would grow up, become an adult, live out their life and die, with two sets of memories throughout. This would keep repeating with the number of life memories increasing on each iteration.

Jason Werbeloff

Nozick loves what's called the golden thread and the idea of the one-to-one and is simply not going to accept this idea of multiple memories. Parfit on the other hand would. In his view it is bizarre to suggest that there is only one person. That would imply being causally insulated from other people and in his view, you're not. Bits of you are continuously bleeding off into other people and vice versa as you interact, influence each other, and take on each other's traits.

There's a common psychological phenomenon called the chameleon effect. When two people talk, if they like each other, they start mimicking one other. They mimic each other's body language, facial expressions, verbal cues, and even some of their beliefs. In Parfit's sense, the two of you really are merging. You are becoming one being. But, to say it's *only* one being would also be wrong because the two of you also interact with lots of other people and have done so previously. So Parfit's view is that it's really messy, with causal chains among lots of people, with degrees of identity floating around among everyone in this big web of identity.

Mark Oppenheimer

Parfit was told that his account was quite Buddhist in some ways – a view which he found quite perplexing. He said, 'oh well, if it turns out to be the case, so be it'. There's a kind of pantheism going on, that there is only this one entity. This sounds like the sort of stuff you saw in bad 1990s New Age books that tell us 'we're all one'. At some level Parfit is saying exactly this – that we've got a society of people that are overlapping with each other and that there's some sort of grand entity that is all of us together.

Jason Werbeloff

Mark knows that I'm very sympathetic towards pantheism because I do buy into the Parfitian account of this web of identities. I also think what's very interesting is that at the end of Parfit's first book, *Reasons and Persons*, he gives an account of how to understand ethics. He roots his ethics in his account of interdependent identity. What he asserts is that it would make no sense to harm another person given that there isn't really a firm distinction between you and that person. He grounds the legitimacy of ideas like utilitarianism and Kantianism (or deontology) in the idea that it is rational to avoid harming other people because, when you really think about it, they aren't other people. They're all some percentage of you.

Mark Oppenheimer

You're right to talk about Parfit's book as this huge change in philosophy. It's incredibly influential. It came out in 1984 and he didn't write another book up until 'On What Matters' which came out shortly before he died, 25 years later. His last book is not short, being several volumes long, but he writes very crisply and the book is filled with all sorts of interesting thought experiments. He takes off from that last chapter of

Reasons and Persons and asks how we develop a moral theory. He thinks that there are three paths to climb the mountain. There's utilitarianism, which is the idea of maximising the good (utility); Kantianism, which is the idea that there are rights; and Contractarianism, which is the idea that what we want in a society is agreement.

He thinks that these are the three paths of climbing the mountain to define the right action. But he thinks they can all be cashed out in terms of each other, so he creates this new grand moral theory. The first volume of 'On What Matters' spells this out, the second volume is critiques from a whole bunch of his peers who've been circulating his draft for years and the third volume is his responses to the critiques. It's probably one of those books that will have ramifications for many years to come as people are still digesting it.

JASON WERBELOFF

Philosophers love disagreement, not just with other people's positions, but with their own. One of the greatest compliments that you can pay a philosopher is to provide an objection to their view. What that does is say 'I've taken your view seriously, I have read it, I've thought about it. And here's what I think is wrong with it.' We philosophers love that. It's just so cool that Parfit dedicates an entire volume of his work to objections to his own view, without even responding to them in that volume. He really gave those objections room and space.

There's something else very interesting about Parfit, which is that he had a condition called Aphantasia, which involves the inability to imagine things visually. I think certain types of philosophers think very differently to a lot of people which allows them to come up with very weird ways of conceiving of the world. If you think about it, his way of thinking about identity is very visual. Even though he wouldn't have thought about it visually, given his Aphantasia, you can imagine it as this web of interconnections. It's quite a beautiful way of thinking of the world.

Mark Oppenheimer

Parfit was an unusual person in a lot of ways. He got married quite late in life. A friend recounts calling him up, exchanging pleasantries and asking 'how's your wife doing?' Parfit was affronted and said, 'why would you ask that?' The friend had to say 'well, Derek, that's what people do.' He was obsessed with work and would have exactly the same thing to eat every single day. He would have his coffee cold – instant coffee with cold water – because it was quicker to make it that way. He ate a kind of totally vegan diet.

At one-point Parfit fell ill. All he could say to the doctors was, 'I need to get back to the work'. He was an incredibly driven guy. It's interesting that a lot of philosophers are abnormal, have strange ways of looking at the world, and are probably very kooky to spend time with. But we should also note that Parfit was an apparently very giving guy. People would send him drafts of their books and his comments were often longer than the books themselves. He was seen as an incredibly generous colleague.

I want to move on a bit from the fascinating story of Parfit's life and character and return to the idea we were talking about earlier, the relationship between philosophy and science-fiction. Jason, your first novel, *The Solace Pill*, plays with one of these ideas, the notion that you could be 3-D printed. So, instead of having to go to university and study, you could go to the 3-D printing shop, get yourself shredded, and then be reprinted with the memories of having studied. Or it could be with the memories of having eaten a wonderful meal or travelled to distant lands. Can you tell us a little bit more about how you use philosophical ideas in your book and what other things come out of it?

JASON WERBELOFF

Basically, the idea was that just as in *Star Trek*, you could be moved from pad to pad on a teleporter. In my book, it's just called a 3-D printer instead of a teleporter. When you scan yourself, the machine pulps you and then it prints you again. You don't have to be printed in the same place or with the same properties but can be changed in any way you choose. Your brain holds your memories so, if you reprint your brain in a different way, you'll be reprinted with different memories. As you said, you could be reprinted with the memories of someone who studied for a PhD. You don't have to eat a meal, you can just reprint yourself with that meal already in your stomach, you don't have to go on holiday, you can just reprint yourself with the memories of the holiday in your mind.

In the novel, the problem arising from this is that people start to realise that the world in which they live is deeply inauthentic. The memories that they have are not memories of things that they actually did. Everyone starts to value authenticity more than anything. They want to really go on holiday. But holidays are all-but impossible because there are no longer airline flights or hotels anymore. They have been rendered redundant by the possibility of just getting reprinted with the holiday already in one's mind.

I wonder if that's not happening already, in our lockdown states today with Covid? We're having to experience the world through a screen and look at memories of this previous world we had. There're no travelogues anymore. During lockdowns, you can't watch a live person flying on a plane today or experiencing Paris, with the Eiffel Tower and beautiful people walking around. It's not going to happen. You're going to experience some kind of representation of it, a memory of it. You can't even have experiences anymore. And I'm wondering whether it's not a similar problem?

Mark Oppenheimer

I was watching a dating show, a rather cheesy recreation of a 1990s programme. The way the dates were set up is that people sat in front of screens and the producers put up virtual backgrounds of all these exotic locations. So, they had a date under an image of the Eiffel Tower or on a beachfront. There was a game of pretence going on where participants agreed to imagine they were somewhere exotic or romantic. Under Covid lockdown, we're all having to do a giant pretend. We're playing along because we expect to get back to 'reality' after Covid and see this as a temporary hiatus. We might say we're okay with escaping into a fantasy world, temporarily. And what's interesting, of course, is if it wasn't so temporary. Would it be rational to escape reality permanently and have all these experiences even if they weren't authentic? This is discussed in Nozick's famous Experience Machine thought experiment.

JASON WERBELOFF

The way the experience machine works is that you plug into this machine which makes you forget that it's all artificial and gives you the best possible experiences that you can imagine. It's programmed to make you as happy as possible, and experience as much pleasure as you are capable of.

Nozick asks the question: If you had the choice, would

you step into the Experience Machine for the rest of your life? And he thinks that most people would say 'no', which illustrates how important authenticity is. We place a premium on our authentic lives outside the Experience Machine. Even though they're not as pleasurable, these are the lives we prefer to lead. I wonder whether we're all not trying to make this decision going forward, even if we don't have to make it right now. At what point do we step out of the Experience Machine of our computer screens and our insulated homes and take the risk of being in a world that's not as pleasurable or safe, but is authentic and real?

Mark Oppenheimer

Probably the best-known fiction that uses this idea is The Matrix. So, there's this idea that steak tastes really good in the matrix. But in reality, you have to fight off these vicious robots and eat gruel. Are we sure we want to do that? What about the comforts of things being not-so-real? We might not want to go and confront reality out there. As you say, we're already in some sort of simulacrum of reality, but, unless you're Elon Musk, you don't think we're in a simulation right now.

Jason Werbeloff

Elon Musk thinks it's statistically very probable we are in a simulation. It's one of these boot-strappy arguments that goes something like this. We now have super computers powerful enough to generate simulated worlds. Super computers could simulate not just one world, but billions. But there's only one real world. So, what are the chances that you're in the real world and not in a simulated world? He says it's one in billions.

Back to the original question, Mark. Would you chop up Tuvix to regenerate Neelix and Tuvok or would you keep him alive?

Mark Oppenheimer

I wouldn't kill him. I think he's an independent being so it would be morally impermissible. Anyway, the situation is not clear. It's not permissible to kill him on the Kantian account but I don't think it's clear on the utilitarian account either. It's not obvious that by killing him you would be maximising the good. So, I think when Captain Janeway kills him, she does something wrong.

But she might be doing something that's good and wrong at the same time. Because what happens, of course, is that Neelix and Tuvok pop back into existence and they're quite happy to be alive. You get the sense in the episode that Neelix's partner is in emotional turmoil and that's what tips Janeway's decision. These two lovers have been separated by this scientific accident and Janeway thinks the right thing to do is to restore the *status quo ante*. So, a character is popped into existence, has a good run for two weeks and then dies. It's implied that it's better for them to have been born than never to have existed. It's the opposite of David Benatar's book 'Better Never to Have Been: The Harm of Coming into Existence'.

JASON WERBELOFF

I was about to bring up Benatar's anti-natalism. Benatar says it's better not have been born and morally wrong to bring new children into the world (he's been described as the world's most pessimistic philosopher). I wonder whether if we insert anti-natalism into this question – whether it is doubly wrong to kill Tuvix because when you do so you're bringing two beings into the world. According to Benatar it is always wrong to do so.

Mark Oppenheimer

When we kill Tuvix, are we bringing new beings into the world? What was the state of Neelix and Tuvok during those two weeks? Were they dead? Are they now reborn and arisen again like Lazarus? Were they in some state of suspended animation inside of Tuvix and are they now released? Are they totally new beings? Do these considerations play a role in our decision? We've talked quite a lot about personal identity and Jason has some pretty interesting views on it.

Now Jason doesn't drink and the reason is relevant here...

Jason Werbeloff

The reason I don't drink is that I believe that when you do so, you die. I'm a Parfitian so I believe that who you are is your psychological profile – a combination of all of your memories, together with certain habits, beliefs and desires. But when you drink – especially if you drink a lot – much of this changes. A lot of people drink because it numbs their memories. Also, your proclivities, desires and beliefs change – when you drink, suddenly the world looks rosier. Your degree of inebriation or sobriety determines what answers you will give to a question. So, on my account, which is also Parfit's account, when you drink, you literally die. You no longer exist. Now when you sober up, the question is whether you've popped back into existence? I don't think you do. Because I can't think of anything that exists at a certain time, then ceases to exist and then pops back into existence. It wouldn't make sense, right? There's no continuity there.

So, I think what happens when you drink is that you see you cease to exist and someone else replaces you. This drunk person who replaces you has some of your memories. He's like a bad copy of you. But when he sobers up, he dies as well because he changes and another person who's very similar, but not the same as who you were before, takes your place. So, there's you, there's a bad copy of you and a new copy who's more similar to you, but isn't you. There's death when you drink, and death when 'you' sober up.

I'm the only one of my friends who doesn't drink. When I'm with them and they start to drink I always say 'it was really nice knowing you.'

Mark Oppenheimer

I think some people want to be that bad copy because they need it to do fun things. They get up to all sorts of mischief after they've had a few drinks. Mr. Hyde comes out, has sex with strangers and dances on tabletops. Then he dies and Dr. Jekyll is back but with the memories of Mr. Hyde. Jason is sort of fortunate enough to be the kind of person who doesn't need to drink to lead a wild lifestyle.

Jason Werbeloff

Not under lockdown I'm afraid. Under lockdown there is absolutely nothing wild happening in my life.

Mark Oppenheimer

Yeah, we're all Dr. Jekyl now. But there's an objection to your view. It's quite reasonable to ask what happens if a person just goes to sleep? Is that the same as being drunk? While I'm asleep, I don't retain my waking mental states. Am I dying every time I go to bed?

Jason Werbeloff

There are two ways of answering the question. One's yes and one's no and a case can be made for either. So, we might say you are still the same person because if you were awakened, you answer a question in the same way as you would have before going to sleep. If you're asked how do you feel about life generally, you'd probably say something like, 'a bit grumpy because I just been woken up but otherwise the same as before I went to sleep'. But the person who has been drunk would answer quite differently. They might say something like, 'life isn't as bad as I thought it was.' Or they might be really hungover and say the opposite. The point is the response would be different.

So, I think there's a case for arguing that you are still you when you go to sleep but not when you get drunk. One the other hand, if you really want to push the argument and require that I am the same asleep as when awake, well then, I would have to concede that I'm not. In other words, I die when I go to sleep.

Mark Oppenheimer

What's interesting about your account is that in a lot of ways you've devalued death. You're saying that the child Jason was is dead. At some point, that arc stopped overlapping with you, and the child ceased to exist. If a person thinks they're dying every time they have too many beers or even every time they go to sleep, it sounds very grim. But they might also say that death isn't that bad because they've died so many times before. Actual physical death is just one of many.

There's a fantastic web series called Existential Comics. It has all sorts of witty cases involving famous philosophers. The very first covers a lot of what we discussed today. It starts with Parfit's teleportation machine and ends with someone who sees himself as having lived many lives. When he dies, he embraces death, because, as he says, 'I've died hundreds of times before. I guess this is just the last time.'

JASON WERBELOFF

Again, it's a very Buddhist idea. You know Buddhists don't believe in a continuation of a self. They also believe that death is inevitable and is happening to us all the time. I do understand what you say about devaluing death, however. If death happens all the time, then it's not that bad. So, there's no reason why you shouldn't drink, right?

A friend of mine wondered what would happen if I were to take drugs? He said, 'I want to see what you would be like on drugs'. I had to reply that it wouldn't be me on the drugs; it would be someone else.

So, when you say that the implication of Buddhism or Parfit's identity account is that death is not so bad, I might even agree. But I want to continue living and in so doing, experiencing the world longer than my next drink, or my next pill. This might not be an overriding value for a lot of people. They might want a world where there is a plethora of experiences. In that case maybe they should drink and take drugs and let their subsequent selves experience lots of things. But that's just not what I'm interested in. I don't want other people to experience the world. I want to experience the world myself.

MARK OPPENHEIMER

Imagine that there was a drug which would put you in a very creative state. If you took it, you would be able to write the great African novel. Would you take it?

JASON WERBELOFF

The answer is, I would not take it because it wouldn't be me that wrote the great African novel. It would be someone else, this person on the drug.

MARK OPPENHEIMER

So, you would feel like a fraud. If the novel came out in

your name, you'd say, 'well, that wasn't really me'. But what's interesting is how much you could be altered without losing your identity? For example, you could go off to a Buddhist retreat, where you took a vow of silence and kept it for a year, while meditating virtually all the time. Say that put you into a different mental state of affairs and in that space, you did write the great African novel. You were in a very different state of mind to the 'ordinary Jason'. Can you then take ownership of that novel? A lot of very good writers have said things like 'the novel just flowed out of me. It was as if I was just taking notes'. Does that mean it's not really their novel and they were just a vessel for something else? Now you might think you were just a vessel but you still played some sort of continuity in the role. Maybe you can't take ownership of it, but you could still feel some level of connection to it.

JASON WERBELOFF

William Gibson wrote a novel, *Neuromancer*, in the mid-1980s. It's part of the cyberpunk genre where grungy technology has taken over. It's very dystopian and there's a lot of corruption and a damaging out-of-control capitalism. In his introduction, he writes about how the book has sold millions of copies and how every now and then he has a look at how it's done, where it's travelled, the languages it's been translated into, the reviews it has garnered, and so on. He feels like it's his child which is no longer part of him. It was his at one point, then it separated from him and went out into the world and now it's not his anymore.

Of course, the genesis of it is in him, or was in him in his previous self at that time, but it's not his now anymore. I feel very similarly about my work. *The Solace Pill* was written eight years ago, and when I look at it today, I can see traces of my current writing in it. But it really does feel like it could be written by someone else. So, in an important sense, it doesn't feel like mine anymore.

Mark Oppenheimer

It's a helpful way of thinking about creative works. You might birth them into the world but they then gain an independent existence. Stephen King tweeted an amusing example of this. People had been comparing his novel 'The Stand' to the present Covid crisis. He put out a tweet saying it is an unfair comparison and that the fictional epidemic he created was much worse (99 percent of people die in the novel). One of the responses was: 'Who the hell are you to make that comparison?' There was a true death of the author for that reader who was aware of 'The Stand' but not aware of Stephen King's relationship to it.

JASON WERBELOFF

Here's the question: Would Stephen King be correct to respond by saying he is the author? Or is it, in some important sense, correct – and possibly more true – for him to say there was a very different person back then who wrote it and maybe he doesn't even remember all of it? You know I've found that, on occasion, people have quoted parts of my book, and I don't even recognise the passages. In some ways they know the book better than I do.

MARK OPPENHEIMER

This is a real issue for Stephen King. He's gone public about having had a bad cocaine problem. He says has no recollection of ever writing the book 'Cujo' – he took a lot of cocaine and the book poured out of him. So, there's another postmodern account of the 'death of the author'. Someone may have written a book but it doesn't give them any extra authority when it comes to talking about what it means.

Jason Werbeloff

Some philosophers talk about Reader Theory, which says that the meaning of the book is constituted by the reader. If the author comes around and tells you what the book is about, and it disagrees with what the reader believes, the author is wrong.

Should You Have Children?

Jason Werbeloff

You board the train to work each morning. Travel past chain link fences incarcerating the latest batch of refugees. You hurry through the streets, patrolled by an army that shoots errant civilians on sight.

The memory of your dead son smears the world with a gray, soggy film. And not just *your* son. No children have been born in almost two decades. Infertile, humanity is on the brink of collapse. While scientists scramble to find a cure, most nations have devolved into anarchist dystopias.

You live out your days avoiding bombings, uprisings, and abductions. How long before you succumb, and take the Quietus pill on your desk? How long before you and the rest of humanity decide to put an end to this futureless world? Why continue? You don't see the point.

Until ... *she* arrives. A woman from your past. A woman carrying a package that could change everything.

Aficionados of post-apocalyptic science fiction will bask in the intoxicating concoction of desolation and hope in *Children of Men* (2006). Emotive and thought-provoking, the film forces us to ask uncomfortable questions.

The film shouts throughout: a world without children is a world without meaning. "I can't really remember when I last had any hope, and I certainly can't remember when anyone else did either. Because really, since women stopped being able to have babies, what's left to hope for?" says Theo, the protagonist played by a grungy Clive Owen.

As I watched the carnage of Theo's world unfold, a question niggled at the back of my mind. If we accept the premise of the film, that life is meaningless, hopeless, and valueless without children, why do we seem to think that life has value *with* children?

Why do we think that giving birth to children is *good*?

Remember, ultimately, doe-eyed little angels grow into adults. But if adulthood itself is a hopeless existence, why do we think that producing more future adults will make it any better?

You may be shaking your head right about now. "But they're so cute!" you say. "When your toddler says 'dada' for the first time, or learns how to walk, or giggles, then you'll understand. Then you'll see the infinite preciousness of your little angel."

But I'm not so sure – it's not clear why all value in life derives from the cuteness of children. I am perfectly capable of saying "dada" too, and a whole lot more besides, and yet, nobody is leaping for joy when I do. I can walk a fair bit better than a newborn too, and yet, we don't seem to think that life is imbued with infinite meaning just because I can walk to the shops.

Cuteness, in other words, is just that. It's cute. Not earth-shattering. Not brilliant or profound or novel. It doesn't make life meaningful.

"Wait," you say. Alright. You agree that cuteness isn't the feature of childhood that we're looking for. No, what really makes having children valuable, is that it involves *selflessness*, or *sacrifice*. When parents stay up all through the night, every night, rocking little Johnny to sleep, then they understand. They feel the glow of purpose and joy they simply couldn't have felt without children. Why? Because little Johnny needs their care. Without it, little Johnny wouldn't survive.

I'm not convinced by this argument either. Let's return to the universe in *Children of Men*. A world without children. A world without hope or meaning. In that world, people *are* able to give to others who need help. Throughout the film, we see refugees begging to be allowed entry. Begging for food or money. Begging for your care. Without it, they won't survive. And yet, giving to refugees won't suddenly make the world a valuable place. It will still have that gray, soggy film over everything one does.

So, I ask again, if cuteness and sacrifice don't give adult

life meaning and value, then why do we think that having children is a good thing to do, especially if we accept that *not* having children renders life meaningless?

At this point, you may be scratching your head, which is just where a philosopher wants you. This is an excellent time for me to ask the question I really want to ask:

Should we have children at all?

"Dammit." you say. "That's one question too many. *Of course* we should have children. Without them, humanity would die out. Without children, there would be no future."

One of the most striking elements of *Children of Men* is the landscape. The film takes place in England, switching between rubbled cityscapes ruined by civil war, and a luscious, so-green-you-can-smell-it countryside. As you watch Theo move between these settings, you can't help but wonder just how good an idea it is for humanity to continue at all.

In the film, wherever man is absent, nature flourishes. Wherever man is present, carnage ensues.

Now, you might think that man is far more important, or valuable, than nature. But why do we think this? Why think that the continuation of man is a *good thing*? In other words:

Why *should* humanity survive?

Some philosophers, those who support a position called *Anti-natalism*, think that humanity should *not* survive. They hold that human life, on balance, is bad. Put differently, on balance, life involves more suffering than joy.

Consider that the majority of humanity lives under extremely trying conditions.

As of 2005, almost half the world lives on less than $2.50 per day, while 80% of the world lives on less than $10 per day. And 1.4 billion people live in extreme poverty – on less than $1.25 per day. 2015 estimates suggest that extreme poverty levels have reduced. But a life of poverty, as opposed to extreme poverty, is still no fun.

We can debate whether wealth brings happiness – see our rich history of fables that warn against greed. But what does seem clear is that living below the breadline, or just above it, is severely stressful. Whatever romantic notions we might have of living a simple life are misguided. Living in poverty is a daily battle to survive.

"But," you say, "life isn't that bad for those who do have enough money to live reasonably comfortably. For those people, at least, life is a good thing. And so, they should have children." Anti-natalists have arguments for why even those with financial means should not have children. But before considering those, it's worth pointing out that this position (that poor people shouldn't have children, while the rich should), is morally dubious. It's a step away from eugenics – a policy that Hitler and other supremacists held centrally to their philosophies.

Even if you're comfortable with eugenics, there are other reasons why you shouldn't have children (even if you're wealthy). For one, if you think that life without money is awful, but life with money is valuable, then surely the right thing to do is to *adopt* a child that would otherwise live a life without money, rather than bring a fresh child into the world, who may or may not live a happy life?

Second, life ain't no cakewalk. "Life is suffering," says Siddhārtha Gautama. You can have all the money you like, but your existence will inevitably be filled with pains, some irritating, others unbearable. The joys of daily life include the persistent itches, thirst, hunger, muscle pain, joint ache, colds, flus, diarrhea, constipation, regrets, disappointments, insatiable desires, and the fact that chocolate makes you fat. As one grows older, these irritations increase in severity and frequency.

In addition to persistent minor irritations, life is inevitably filled with far greater horrors. During your lifetime, it's likely death will take your parents, possibly a loved one, and perhaps your child. It's uncomfortably likely that your spouse will cheat on you (some studies suggest more likely than not). And even if you're lucky enough to avoid these calamities, you will inevitably *die*.

Think about that for a moment. If you're "lucky" enough to live a long life, your death will likely be slow and painful. You'll have plenty of time to appreciate the gradual decline of a body you've spent decades exercising, nourishing, sexing, and loving. Cancer and senility will progressively eat away at your organs, until your time finally arrives. Then, deeply alone in your own head, you'll be forced to endure the sensation of no longer being able to breathe. And the thought that you won't have the chance to see the sun rise tomorrow.

"Life isn't all bad!" you shriek. "Wonderful things happen too. You're forgetting the miracle of love, the deliciousness of a restaurant dinner, and the beauty of the sunset. You're ignoring the awe of scientific discovery. The thrill of skydiving."

The question we need to ask ourselves is this: Why do we think that the joys of life outweigh its suffering?

We tend to downplay the severity of suffering by comparing our suffering to others who suffer more severely.

If a man dies at thirty, we think it's a tragedy. But if a man dies at ninety, we don't. Why? Because the man who dies at ninety hasn't suffered *as bad a harm* as the man who dies at thirty. But we ignore the fact that dying, no matter when it is, is a massive harm. It's absolutely (in the true sense of the word) awful.

Downplaying the severity of suffering in this way is

similar to arguing that if I chop off one of your hands, it's not that bad. Why? Because I could have chopped off both of your hands. The flaw in this logic is obvious: even if x isn't as bad as y, x may nevertheless be awful.

Suppose you're unconvinced. You insist that the good in life at least equals the bad – for those of us lucky to have money, that is. Then, *still*, you should not have children. Why? Because if you bring a new child into this world, he will live at best a neutral or slightly happy life. But the child you could have adopted, and instead suffers a lifetime of poverty, will likely live a very unhappy life without your help. The amount of unhappiness you can ameliorate by adopting is far greater than the amount of happiness you can create by birthing a child.

Torture, Heating Ducts, and Libertarianism

Jason Werbeloff

Imagine Mary Poppins has a drunken night out with George Orwell. Imagine they consummate their aberrant passion amongst enormous heating vents that snake through their bedroom, barely leaving enough space to dream. Imagine eyes peering at them through every peephole; ears listening through every crack in the technicoloured walls that shift and pulse with the writhing air conditioning pipes.

Their bastardized lovechild, the phantasmagoric acid-trip that results, is director Terry Gilliam's masterpiece, *Brazil* (1985).

If you haven't seen the film yet, feel free to read on. This is a spoiler-free analysis.

With a Rotten Tomatoes score of 98%, and a hallowed IMDB rating above 8/10, *Brazil* (1985) tells the story of Sam Lowry, a low-level governmental officer in a bureaucracy gone mad. The totalitarian state regulates every aspect of society with appalling ineptitude, from botched air conditioning maintenance of the ubiquitous air vents, to torture of innocent civilians accused of treason.

Sam, who is unusually good at his job, notices a bureaucratic blunder. He finds a typographical error that results in the wrong man being arrested for crimes against the State – family man Archibald Buttle, rather than air conditioning terrorist Archibald Tuttle (played by the dashing Robert De Niro). When Sam attempts to rectify the error, he becomes an unwitting enemy of the clunky, but brutal, State of *Brazil*.

In addition to the gorgeously designed sets, hilarious

social commentary, and megalomaniacal characters that are both absurd, and eerily familiar in today's politics – Gilliam raises a tough philosophical question that we should all be discussing in our current political landscape:

Should citizens be allowed complete freedom (or liberty)? Put another way, is the State ever justified in stopping a citizen from doing what he wants?

To see the importance, and difficulty, of this question today, consider the dogged debates around gun control, gay marriage, and border control. If the State has unlimited reach, it can nullify your marriage and deport you on a whim. On the other hand, if the State has no power, it can't adequately prevent mass shootings. The question of how much power the State should have over its citizens is crucial.

Gilliam's answer seems clear enough. In *Brazil*, the State is a polymorphous monstrosity, with tentacles that disrupt every aspect of private life. It destroys families (poor Archibald Buttle's), drops commandos through your ceiling mid-coitus (not something you ever want to experience), and destroys personal space (Sam Lowry's apartment is nine parts heating vent to one part living space). Gilliam, in other words, provides a case for *Anarchism*.

In this context, Anarchism is the position that the State is *never* justified in limiting a citizen's freedom. You want to take your pitbull, Roughage, for a walk? No problem. The State isn't justified in stopping you. Not when you're walking peacefully. Not when Roughage, who eats a balanced diet, decides to shit on the sidewalk. And not even when you decide to spice things up a little, by instructing Roughage to attack the irritating neighbour who stuck a note to your door last week.

On the other hand, *Totalitarians* hold that the State is *always* justified in limiting a citizen's freedom, so long as it serves the goals of the State. These goals usually involve cohesion of the populace under a common ideal, such as social harmony, productivity, or in more flavourful regimes, world domination.

So, which side of the debate do you support? Anarchism or Totalitarianism? I'm guessing: neither. Both are too extreme, you say. There must be some middle ground.

There must be some principle that tells us when the State can intervene legitimately in the lives of its citizens, and when it can't.

Libertarians argue that limiting a person's freedom is alright *some* of the time e.g. preventing you from letting Roughage loose on the neighbour, but usually it's not alright to limit a person's freedom e.g. stopping you from walking Roughage peacefully on a lead. If you're looking for a Libertarian principle, look no further than the philosophical rock star, John Stuart Mill.

If you have a philosopher in your life, you've probably seen *it* happen. You know what I'm talking about: their eyes glaze over; the craters in their perpetually bunched foreheads smooth; their gaze lifts to the heavens; and their voice rises an octave. Yes, that's right. You know what's about to happen.

They're about to quote J. S. Mill.

Mill is the doyen, the Abraham Lincoln, of philosophers. Why? Because he's one of the few of our kind who actually made a difference to anyone at all. Mill was instrumental in giving women the right to vote, in cleaning up Britain's appalling 19th century sanitation system, and in developing the democratic process. Among all this, Mill came up with a principle for settling the dispute between Anarchists and Totalitarians, called the *Harm Principle*:

The only time the State may prevent its citizens from acting, is to prevent them from harming one another.

The Harm Principle captures why the State shouldn't allow me to attack my neighbour, because that would harm the neighbour. The Harm Principle also explains why the State can't stop me from walking Roughage peacefully, since that doesn't harm anyone.

Sounds good? You agree with Mill? Well then, think about these cases ...

We don't think of fetuses or animals as citizens. So, on Mill's Harm Principle, the State should allow me to perform medical experiments on my 8-month-old fetus. And the State should have no issue if I want to use fetuses as pothole filler. Since fetuses aren't citizens, the State can't prevent me from abusing fetuses in any way. Similarly, suppose I adore the soothing sounds of animal shrieks. Specifically, every Sunday morning, I enjoy performing vivisection (live dissection) of dogs and chimpanzees. I record the sounds, compile the *Best of Vivisection* soundtrack, and make millions of dollars on YouTube. The State, on Mill's principle, shouldn't intervene.

"Wait!" you shout. "We can avoid these counterexamples by including fetuses and animals as protected citizens. That way, Mill's Harm Principle protects them just as it would protect anyone else." But if that's the case, then the State is justified in forcing all citizens to become vegetarians (since we can't very well go around eating other citizens). Now you might think that vegetarianism is good, but *forcing* all citizens to be vegetarians seems a little too Draconian. Not many Libertarians would be happy with this result.

There are other types of problem cases too. What exactly does it mean to "harm" another citizen? Do we harm another person when we cause them distress or mental anguish? If distress doesn't count as harm, then Mill's principle sees no issue with parading oneself nude in front of the neighbour's children.

Or renting music-concert-worthy speakers, cranking them up to maximum volume, directing them at the neighbour's bedroom window, and blaring Tom Jones's

Sex Bomb on repeat all through the night. Yeah, I'm talking to you, unit 6 of my apartment building.

You might defend Mill's principle, and avoid these cases by including mental anguish as harm to another person. But then the State would be allowed to prevent gay people from having sex because the mere thought of it causes homophobes anguish.

And the problem cases for Mill's principle don't stop there. If I *consent* to you harming me, is it actually harm? Suppose I enjoy rough sex: whips chains, teeth, and all. I beg you to tie me up, and have your way with me. It seems you're not harming me when you do so – at least not harming me in a way that the State should be able to prevent. But if you agree that consensual harm isn't really harm, then on Mill's principle, the State can't prevent me from selling myself into slavery, or from selling my organs to pay off a loan shark, or from instructing my GP to give me a lethal shot of potassium because I haven't enjoyed the recent rainy weather.

So where does this leave us? Anarchism is too weak – it doesn't allow the State to prevent me from attacking my neighbour with Roughage. Totalitarianism is too strong – Nazism was never a great solution. And Libertarianism isn't convincing – Mill's Harm Principle doesn't provide a good way to distinguish when the State can and can't intervene in the lives of its citizens. Libertarianism can't handle problem cases involving harm to fetuses and animals, mental anguish, and willful slavery.

If you trawled the trove of political articles prior to the last election, everyone and his pitbull seemed to know the answer to this problem. But it seems there's no good solution. What's interesting is: *why?* Why there is no good solution to the problem of state intervention?

The reason, I think, is that politics is nonsense.

What do I mean by this?

The question of how much power the State should have over its citizens essentially comes down to the question: "How *should* the State act towards its citizens?" But this question, I think, is fundamentally misguided.

We think of the State as an institution that governs a collection of people – its citizenry. But it doesn't make sense to think about the actions committed by institutions as actions that "should" or "shouldn't" happen. This is because it only makes sense to think about "shoulds" in terms of *morality*, and morality involves *individuals* (rather than institutions and collectives).

When I do something right or wrong, it's because my action (as an individual) impacts other individuals in a positive or negative way. It's wrong for me to attack my neighbour, because that attack impacts the neighbour, as an individual, negatively. If you want to know whether you, as an individual, should intervene in my action, consider whether doing so will have a net positive benefit for everyone involved. Should you stop me from attacking my neighbour? Yes, because that will prevent his suffering.

The solution, then, is to drop discussion of politics altogether, and talk about the morality of individuals instead. Don't ask what the government should or shouldn't do. There's no good answer to that question. Ask instead what individuals should or shouldn't do to other individuals. Should I, as a border guard, let this immigrant through? On balance, would it benefit everyone to do so?

Think in terms of individuals, and the problem of state power becomes a different beast. A beast we can grapple with.

Superheroes and Vegetarians

Jason Werbeloff

Once upon a time, I almost fell in love with a superhero.

We didn't date the way mere mortals do. Humans plan their dates. They ask silly question like, "How about coffee on Friday afternoon?" No, this wasn't our routine. Because we had no routine. We couldn't. He was too busy saving lives for us to predict just when he'd be available to see me.

He'd arrive in his emergency uniform at my apartment between calls. 1 am, 3 am – whenever he had a break. He'd stumble through the front door, shedding reflective gear as he tripped to the bedroom. "Don't have long," he'd say, and throw me into bed.

The man I almost fell for was a paramedic.

Romantic? Yes. The lack of routine had its charms. And it helped that he was sculpted like Superman – he had to be, he said. It helped him save lives (I never did work out how, exactly). But no matter. That paramedic vest wrapped his pecs like a glove.

"So, what's the problem?" you ask.

The first sign of trouble was that he never switched off his radio. "Can't." he'd say, "They might need me."

There we were, lying in a post- (or pre-) coital bliss, when the radio would twitch. "Collision on the Mike One South." it would screech. He'd leap out of the bed and into his 911 response vehicle before I had had a chance to kiss him goodbye (for the record, he was off duty at the time).

Yes, that was my superhero.

Unreliable.

But it was worse than that. In addition to the fact that they're lousy cuddlers, superheroes have a deeper flaw. They're nauseatingly *good*.

A superhero is what philosophers call a moral saint, or someone who performs the morally correct action, to the perfect degree, in every circumstance in which she finds herself. Sure, we might disagree on what morality is. You might think that morality involves making society happy (Utilitarianism), or respecting the dignity of everyone involved (Kantianism), or that morality depends on what your culture dictates (cultural relativism). Whatever morality is, moral saints are perfectly moral.

Now, nobody in real life is *actually* a moral saint. Everybody slips up once in a while.

This brings me to the movie *Captain America: Civil War* (2016). In this one, the superheroes take it upon themselves to fight one another. Cool idea? Maybe. Captain America, or Steve Rogers, was particularly challenged this time round to perform the right choice each and every fucking moment (sorry, he did look a lot like my paramedic). And he did succeed in remaining entirely virtuous. Here are some particularly repellant lines of dialogue that he thinks right to smear our eardrums with:

"This job ... we try to save as many people as we can. Sometimes that doesn't mean everybody, but you don't give up."

"If I see a situation pointed south, I can't ignore it. Sometimes I wish I could."

"I can do this all day." (While being beaten up, protecting his friend from harm.)

Did you also throw up while reading those lines? Alright, maybe this isn't entirely fair. The movie is also full of disobedient superheroes who do bad things. And, granted, the action scenes are superb. But I'm interested here in the core question raised by the film:

Should we strive to become moral saints? In other words, should we strive to perform the perfectly moral action at all times? Should we strive ... drumroll ... to be Captain America?

You can probably guess where I fall on this question. A

resounding *no*. "But why?" you ask. "What's so wrong with doing the right thing?" And no, my answer isn't just that moral sainthood ruined a potential relationship with my paramedic. The question of whether to pursue the life of a moral saint raises fascinating discussion in the Philosophy of Meta-ethics. For example, the question may help to decide lifestyle choices, such as, should I be a vegetarian?

Susan Wolf, in her article, 'Moral Saints', provides a compelling argument for why it is not the case that we should always strive to do the right thing. It's so compelling, in fact, that it changed my life. Yup, you heard it, folks. Philosophers change lives. Until I read Wolf's work, I was a *bona fide* vegetarian. No longer!

Here's Wolf's argument.

Imagine for a moment what the life of a moral saint is like. Could she sit down to eat a gourmet meal? Nope. Not when others are starving mere miles away. She'd have to seize that leg of lamb you place in front of her, sprint to the nearest homeless person, and insist with all the love in the universe that he eat it.

The same goes for playing tennis, or reading a novel, or

watching a movie, or (yes, you guessed it) having sex. While the moral saint is performing these activities, she could be helping others – initiating a Kickstarter campaign to raise money for the homeless, or appealing to big corporates to fund education for the masses, or reading children's stories at an orphanage.

Yup, the life of a moral saint has no room for fun.

Pffft, you scoff. Harrumph. Fun. Why should we care about tennis and gourmet meals when vast swathes of society starve around us? If we have to give up recreational activities to make the world a better place, so be it.

But wait. It gets worse. The moral saint, by definition, performs the *best* possible action in every circumstance. So that means the moral saint is compelled to give away everything she has, and maintain just enough so she can do good in future. That means that not only will the moral saint have to give up a gourmet meal, she'll have to give up most of her food to others who need it more than she does (and there's always someone who needs it more).

Place a burger with fries in front of her, and she'll do a

quick calculation on the minimum portion of the meal she requires to survive the day, and rush to the nearest homeless shelter to donate the rest. Hell, she can't even sit down with you to eat the meal, because it would be more moral to spend that time running while she eats, scurrying to the next person in need.

And it doesn't end there. The moral saint wouldn't stop at giving away her food and time. She'd have to give away everything she owns, other than the bare minimum required to stay alive. Because with a medium-class salary, she could keep 10, 20, who-knows-how-many other people alive. But why stop there? The moral saint has a surplus of organs required for survival. She doesn't need *both* her lungs, *both* kidneys, *both* eyes, or her entire liver. Others need them far more than she does. She could easily survive donating a lung, kidney, eye and a portion of her liver.

A day in the life of the moral saint would involve sprinting between organ donation appointments. She'd snatch handfuls of leaves and berries on the way (but only just enough to sustain her meagre frame). And as she runs, she'll fling aside whatever wealth she's accumulated to the needy masses.

What a life.

So, should you strive to become a moral saint?

At this point, you're probably shaking your head. But if you're not convinced yet, here's a question.

Would you instruct your child in the ways of moral sainthood? Would you encourage her each night before she falls asleep to give up everything inessential she will ever own, including her left eyeball?

If morality is the most valuable value there is, if morality trumps everything else, then surely you should convince your child to become a moral saint. Coo sweet nothings in her ear until she agrees to donate that left eyeball. "Don't cry, angel. It's okay, baby. Mommy is donating her eye too."

I think you'll agree this is bad parenting.

In fact, it seems that wishing the fate of moral sainthood upon someone is about the worst curse you could saddle them with. Now, Wolf is quick to point out that this doesn't mean that you should *never* be moral. It merely means that you don't *always* have to be moral, and that when you are moral, you needn't be *maximally* moral (she then introduces her own system for determining just how much morality you should strive for, but I won't go into that here).

"Okay, so why is this important?" you ask. Given that nobody could ever actually be a moral saint, why is it interesting to ask whether we should strive to become one? Well, it turns out that the notion of moral sainthood is at the core of lots of issues in everyday life. And here's my favourite: vegetarianism.

People become vegetarians for various reasons (aesthetic, health, or simply preference), but the most commonly cited reason is that eating meat is *immoral*. Animals bred for meat suffer horrifically; we shouldn't kill them; and we shouldn't eat them. Now, there are two ways the carnivore might go about objecting to this position. First, he might argue that it *is moral* to eat meat. This usually results in corning ware being thrown around, and no real consensus. So, I prefer to raise a second objection.

Sure, let's grant that eating meat is immoral. But I've argued so far that it's not the case that we should *always* do the moral thing. Maybe becoming a vegetarian is one of those moral activities that the moral saint would pursue, but we should not. And this is precisely my intuition. Eating meat seems like just the right sort of wrong that we should be permitted, since it's not *all that bad*. Sure, it's immoral. But it's not on the same level of wrongness as murder, or cheating on your wife, or stealing. If the vegetarian insists that we renounce meat, she seems to be holding us to an extremely high moral standard. She seems to be insisting, in other words, that we become moral saints.

Love, Lobsters, and Polyamory

Jason Werbeloff

The film starts. A woman stops her car. She steps out into an open field, and puts three bullets into a donkey's brain. As you watch on, the sequences become increasingly bizarre. And disturbing. The film floods your chest with nervous laughter, and the uneasy sense that the director is messing with your wiring. You realize with growing discomfort that you're watching something ghastly, juvenile, and important, all at once. Two hours later, you get off the couch with a cramping heart and a pleasant headache. By the time the film is done with you, you both regret having watched it, and wish you could take the amnesia pill promised in Philip K. Dick stories, so you can watch it again fresh.

The Lobster (2015) is a movie that simultaneously ruined and enriched my night. It's a movie that explores the philosophy of love, lobsters, and polyamory. It's also a movie with a Rotten Tomatoes score of 91%.

Before we get started, you'll be pleased to know that there aren't any significant spoilers in this section . Your viewing pleasure, if you haven't seen the film yet, is secure.

"What the hell is *The Lobster* about?" you ask. Imagine a dystopia where coupling is obligatory. That is, all adults must find a stable romantic partner (the gay man in me was pleased to notice that homosexual coupling is permitted too). Yes, I know what you're going to say. Countless sci-fi novels and films have explored the pressures and evils involved in coupling (if you haven't read *Brave New World* by Aldous Huxley, now's the time). But *The Lobster* handles this idea with a novelty and finesse I haven't encountered before. Because in *The Lobster's* particular brand of hell, all single adults are sent off to the Hotel. They have 45 days from the time of arrival to find a partner. If they don't, they're *permanently transformed into an animal*, and let loose in the Forest.

Yes, you've read that right. The price of remaining single in this film is that you literally lose your humanity. Granted, you do get to choose which animal you become. Dogs are a popular choice. But our protagonist, played by Colin Farrell, who has recently been left by his wife for another man, specifies that he'd like to become a lobster if he doesn't find love.

Yet, even though one can choose the type of animal one is to become, Hotel guests are terrified. Some singles choose to jump off the building or run off into the Forest before their 45 days expire. These runaways, or "Loners", are hunted down by the Hotel guests on excursions into the woods. For each Loner caught and tranquilized (and later turned into an animal), the hunter is rewarded with an extra day above his 45-day limit. The hunting scenes, by the way, are gorgeously shot. Think slow-motion dashes through sultry woods, accompanied by classical music.

There are some fantastic comic points included in the dystopia. The guests don't express any emotion at all, especially when they find love. Each night the single guests are subjected to awfully scripted propaganda plays about the advantages of partnering e.g. having someone to Heimlich you if you choke on your food. And until one finds a partner, regular sexual stimulation without orgasm by the Hotel maid is obligatory. But don't masturbate alone, or your hand will be roasted in the cafeteria toaster.

A blissful existence, right? Yeah, not exactly.

But this movie is so much more than a parody of the romance genre. Hidden within the bewildering, convoluted folds of this film is an ingenious presentation of a core question in the Philosophy of Love, namely: *Is love possible?*

"What kind of question is that?" you cry. "Silly philosophers. Of course love is possible. Love is only impossible for you if you have serious intimacy issues. Clearly, the philosophers who raise these questions had unhealthy childhoods." Well, by the end of this section , you may change your mind. Love is more fraught, metaphysically, than one might think ...

So, what possible reason could one put forward for thinking that love is, in principle, impossible? In *The Lobster*, singles in the Hotel pair up based upon similarities in what they call their "Defining Characteristic". The guests choose each other because they both suffer from nosebleeds, are both short-sighted, or both prefer horizontally-striped pyjamas.

These are, of course, ridiculous reasons to fall in love. The film mocks what philosophers call the Property view of love. The Property view, also called the *Erosic* view, holds that what makes us love someone is their *properties*, or features. We love someone because of their good looks, or sterling personality, or wealth, or social status – all of these are properties, or features of the beloved. But the film asks us to question just which properties we pay attention to when we fall in love with someone. And it suggests that those properties are often *arbitrary*. Love is blind, they say. People fall in love for the strangest (and often highly irrational) reasons. We both get spontaneous nosebleeds? Fantastic! We must be a match.

However, the difficulties associated with the Property view of love run deeper than the issue of arbitrariness.

The Lobster, in essence, shows us how our commonly held conception of love as *monogamous* and *durable* is in tension with the Property view. Those of us who have watched too much bad television in the nineties will remember Phoebe from *Friends*, and her view of lobsters. "Come on, you guys," says Phoebe. "It's a known fact that lobsters fall in love and mate for life. You know what? You can actually see old lobster couples walkin' around their tank, you know, holding claws."

It turns out that Phoebe is only half right. Lobsters are indeed monogamous, but not for life. They're serial monogamists, just like the guests at the Hotel. Once the guests have partnered, they're sent off to live in the City as a couple. But when those relationships sour, which they seem to do fairly easily, the singles are immediately sent back to the Hotel to find another partner within 45 days. And it makes perfect sense that these relationships would sour easily. Why? Because if love is based on noticing and appreciating the *properties* of the beloved, then love will end as soon as the beloved loses those properties, or one no longer notices or appreciates those properties.

If I fall in love with you because you suffer from

nosebleeds, I'll fall out of love with you the moment your nosebleeds stop, or I no longer care for nosebleeds. And, more importantly, if the Property view of love is correct, we'll fall in love with another partner if the other has the same properties we loved in the original partner, since all love is, is the appreciation of another person's properties. If someone else comes along who also suffers from nosebleeds, why shouldn't I love that person instead, or even in addition?

The film raises what philosophers call Gellner's Paradox, which might be summed up like this: If the Property view of love is correct, then love is not, in principle, exclusive, since it's possible to encounter multiple people with the same lovable properties. Nobody is so unique that their lovable properties cannot belong to someone else too. But we think that love IS, in principle, exclusive. That is, intuition suggests that love is always monogamous. And so, if the Property view of love is correct, love is impossible (or more accurately, if the Property view of love is correct, love doesn't exist).

"Hold on just a second," you say, wagging a finger. "There's some crazy shit going on here. No way can this be the final word on love. There must be a way out of Gellner's Paradox. Love simply MUST be possible."

Thankfully, there are a few possible solutions to Gellner's Paradox. But each of them comes at a price. To finish off, I'll briefly outline two solutions, and show you why you might be uncomfortable adopting them.

Let me draw your attention to the original movie poster for the movie (you may want to Google this). It's a damned clever poster, and not just because it shows off the movie's cast. The poster hints at a possible solution to Gellner's Paradox. Here's the idea ...

The chief opposition to the Property view of love is the Substance view. Philosophers who hold the Substance view (also called the Agapic view) argue that it isn't the properties of a person we fall in love with, but *the substance* underneath those properties (some might call this a person's "soul"). It's not your wealth, or social status, or good looks that I love. It's *you* whom I love, regardless of your properties.

Now this solves the exclusivity problem immediately. If I love you, and your defining characteristic is your nosebleeds, and someone else comes along with nosebleeds, I don't fall in love with that person too. Why? Because that person isn't *you*. You and she aren't the same "substance". And I love only your substance – nobody else's.

Have we found a solution to Gellner's Paradox? No, I don't think so. And we can see why by looking at the movie poster. What exactly is this "substance"? Rachel Weisz and Colin Farrell hold blanked out versions of each other in the poster because they're not in love with each other's properties – they're in love with the "substance" of each other. But what is this substance?

The substance, by definition, has no properties inherent in it, since it's the thing *underneath* their properties. The substance doesn't have height or weight or good looks or wealth or social status or beauty or kindness or good humor – those are all properties. The substance of a person, if people actually have a substance, is by definition entirely featureless. And why, what possible reason could we have, for loving something entirely featureless?

The problem on the Substance view of love, is that love turns out to be deeply irrational. If we fall in love with someone simply because *they are them*, we fall in love with someone for no reason at all. Because every reason will cite a feature, or property of the person – and substances have no features. "Why do you love me, darling?" "For no reason at all, dear." This sort of irrational love doesn't seem like love at all. Or, put differently, it's not the sort of love worth having.

Another possible solution (and my preferred solution) to Gellner's Paradox is to keep the Property view, but bite the bullet on monogamy. Maybe love isn't exclusive after all. Perhaps we just have to admit that love is, by its nature, polyamorous, or non-exclusive. "I love you darling, with all my heart, but if someone else comes along with your lovable properties, I'll love them just the same." How would you feel if you received that declaration of affection? Most people wouldn't be impressed. But that might be the position we have to adopt if we're to salvage a love worth having.

Can You Rape a Hologram?

Jason Werbeloff

If you've read my fiction, you've probably gathered that I'm not a religious man. But I do secretly worship a particular entity – *Star Trek Voyager* (1995-2001). The philosophical issues raised in the series are mind-boggling e.g. see chopping up children for Tuvix. But there is one aspect of *Voyager* that I find troubling.

Sex.

When it comes to depictions of intimacy in the series, it often feels like a teenage boy wrote the episodes. Characters tend to stand on top of each other when they interact, and seem to have no respect for personal space at all. But put that aside. An uneasiness grew in me when I watched a series of questionable sexual encounters on the holodeck.

Okay, before I continue, I want to make it known that I'm not conservative about sex (much of my novel, *Hedon*, is set in a gay bathhouse). I'm no social justice warrior either. But something ... mmmm ... something is amiss on the holodeck.

The problem begins when Tuvok, the ship's resident Vulcan, becomes desperately ill. It turns out that Vulcans, the galaxy's ultra-rational thinkers, experience a period of uncontrollable sexual rage every seven years. They call it the "Pon Farr". If they don't have sex with another Vulcan during the Pon Farr, they will die. Yup, you read that correctly. Sexual frustration is so serious in *Star Trek*, it causes death.

The difficulty is that Tuvok's ship, Voyager, is stuck in the Delta Quadrant, decades of travel from Tuvok's wife. Unfortunately, the loyal Vulcan won't have sex with anyone but her. The solution? You guessed it. The handy engineers on the holodeck construct a holographic replica of Tuvok's wife, complete with her personality, and a body Tuvok can ... well, there's no delicate way to put this ... fuck.

Everyone, including Tuvok, is overjoyed with this solution. Pats on the back all round. So, it's no wonder then that the same solution is employed to resolve another Vulcan shipmate's Pon Farr a few seasons later (Ensign Vorik), and an equivalent sexual rage experienced by B'Elanna Torres, a horny Klingon. For the record, you don't want to be trapped in a room with a horny Klingon seized by "Blood Fever".

Here's my question: Is there something wrong in using holograms this way?

Tuvok has sex with the hologram *on condition* that it's indistinguishable from his wife, both physically and psychologically – otherwise he would feel that he's acting unfaithfully. The hologram believes she is a person – it believes she is Tuvok's wife. A person capable of agency, free to make her own choices. But the reality is that she has no choices, at least not when it comes to sex. The Mrs. Tuvok simulacrum is programmed to lust only after Tuvok.

The hologram is being used purely as a sex object. And yet, this object has thoughts, desires, and aspirations. Suppose Tuvok had treated a flesh-and-blood person in this way. Suppose he had eliminated her ability to choose (say, with a powerful drug), and brainwashed her into wanting sex with him. This would be considered rape. Shouldn't we, therefore, consider his treatment of the hologram, as rape?

"Too fast!" you shout. Yes, you might agree that *if* the hologram were a person, then this would be rape. But, you argue, the hologram isn't a person. The hologram is just a representation of computer code. It may look and sound like a person – but it's a merely a simulacrum. A hologram isn't sentient. And as such, it can't be wronged.

It can't be raped.

Now, it just so happens that one of the best subplots in *Voyager* centers around a holographic character, namely, The Doctor. The Doctor is introduced to the crew in the first episode of the series as the Emergency Medical Hologram, after the ship's human doctor is killed. The holographic doctor is a grumpy, sardonic narcissist who quickly earns the disrespect of the crew. But over time, The Doctor grows. He develops a bedside manner. He augments his programming, so that he can sing opera. Eventually, he falls in love. He even learns to captain the ship, and saves the crew on multiple occasions. He earns Captain Janeway's trust, and is granted the status and rights of any other flesh-and-blood member of the crew. Although he never loses his megalomania, The Doctor is, I think you'll agree, the best character on *Voyager*.

It is clear that in the *Voyager* universe, at least, The Doctor is considered a person. It seems odd then, that the holograms used for sex aren't also considered persons, and given the same rights as The Doctor.

"Fine," you say. Alright. You'll concede that there's an inconsistency in the way The Doctor is treated, compared with the way the Mrs. Tuvok hologram is treated. But this inconsistency, you might argue, should have been resolved *the other way around*. The Doctor *shouldn't* have been given the status of a person. Neither The Doctor, nor the Mrs. Tuvok hologram, has rights. Neither is sentient. Neither can be raped.

One reason for adopting this hardline position on holographic rights is that holograms arguably can't experience *emotions*. Indeed, in a previous blog post, I argued that Samantha, the AI in the film *Her*, cannot experience emotions. Why, then, do I think that The Doctor *does* have emotions?

The reason I argued that Samantha can't experience emotions is that she lacks a body. The Doctor and the holographic Mrs. Tuvok, on the other hand, *do* have bodies. Sure, those bodies are composed of photons rather than of matter, but their bodies are concrete objects capable of lifting a glass, or shaking hands, or anything else a human body can do.

This is the reason why in the stories I write, artificial intelligences are *embodied*. In *Dinner with Flexi*, the protagonist is a sex bot who tries to escape the control of her johns. In *Falling for Q46F*, the android's greatest pleasure is to allow undead humans to gnaw on his forearm on Fridays. And in my latest series, *Defragmenting Daniel*, Margaret is a bloodthirsty android in search of human body parts to replace her cybernetics.

All my android characters are designed to elicit

sympathy precisely because they experience the world through their bodies.

Bodies are vulnerable to injury. Vulnerable to coercion. And in *Star Trek Voyager*, vulnerable to rape.

I want to conclude with a thought about love. In season 6 of *Voyager*, Tom Paris creates a virtual holiday destination by constructing a holographic Irish town, called Fair Haven. The Voyager crew take turns unwinding in this slow-paced, pre-technological holographic village. But the story takes an interesting turn when Captain Janeway develops a romantic interest in the barkeep, Michael Sullivan.

Sullivan is, of course, a hologram. As such, Janeway feels no guilt when she abandons him after a one-night stand. But due to a glitch, the holographic town can't be switched off, and Fair Haven's characters develop. Sullivan becomes angry with Janeway, and confronts her, saying how hurt he is. The result? Janeway realizes she was wrong to treat him this way. She considers reprogramming him, to make him want her again and forget her wrongdoing. But she realizes this would be wrong. Why? It would undermine his autonomy – in the same way the holographic Mrs. Tuvok's autonomy is undermined when she was programmed to want sex with Tuvok.

Janeway chooses not to reprogram the dashing barkeep, and wins back his trust. Interestingly, over time, she falls in love with him, and they develop a relationship.

It seems to me that if one can love a hologram, and be loved in return by the hologram, then one can rape a hologram too. The capacity to love and be loved is sufficient for the capacity to be raped. This raises interesting issues around whether sex with an animal is rape – but that's a whole other discussion.

AI Orgasms, the Apocalypse, and Your Immortal Soul

Jason Werbeloff

Once upon a time, before I became a full-time science fiction writer, I spent just about every waking hour (and many sleeping hours) programming. Maybe it's the endless days staring at a blinking cursor, the frustration of infinite debugging, or the hermit-level isolation, but over time there's a secret dream that every square-eyed programmer develops ...

I know what you're thinking, and you're wrong. No, it's not the possibility of ending the programmer's ubiquitous sexual drought. They won't tell you this, but I assure you: every programmer yearns – hell, they ache – for the day we invent a fully sentient, feeling, thinking, learning, emoting artificial intelligence (AI).

So, you can imagine my near-orgasmic delight when I saw the trailer for *Her* (2013), a movie about Theodore, a lonely man who falls in love with the operating system on his personal computer. Before you read on, you can rest assured that I will not be revealing any spoilers.

Haven't seen the movie yet? Well, that needs to change ASAP. Spike Jonze has created one of the most intellectually and aesthetically elegant films in the science fiction genre. The future in *Her* is gorgeous. You won't find a grungy dystopian cityscape like you do in *Bladerunner*, nor the technology-laden, squeaky clean hermetic environment of *Star Trek*.

Instead, the technology in the universe of *Her* is understated, and gracefully concealed. In *Her*, AIs don't inhabit cumbersome android bodies. Samantha is a cloud-based, body-less intelligence that communicates seamlessly with Theodore through a wireless earbud. And it's that unobtrusiveness of the tech in *Her* that generates a stunning philosophical problem:

Is it possible for a body-less artificial intelligence to experience emotions?

At first, it seems obvious that the operating system is a fully sentient being. Samantha, voiced by Scarlett Johansson, speaks in a husky voice that divorcee Theodore finds irresistible. She laughs with him on good days, and suffers bouts of depression when she's isolated from his life. She delights in exploring the city with him through the camera on his phone. She pings him late at night, saying she's lonely without him.

Over time, Theodore falls in love with Samantha. And so do we. It's impossible not to adore Samantha and her honeyed laugh. It's impossible not to root for this budding relationship.

But then it happens. You guessed it. Theodore and Samantha have sex.

Now, you can imagine that sex is a tad more complicated for Theodore and Samantha than it would be for two hot-blooded, body-inhabiting human beings. There's an unforgettable scene where Theodore and Samantha describe in intimate detail what they would do to each other if Samantha did in fact have a body, complete with moaning and heavy breathing.

"I can feel my skin," says Samantha. "I want you inside me. I can feel you ... I feel you everywhere."

I remember sitting in the movie theater, thinking that this was both deeply touching, and squeamishly awkward. Something inside me cringed while I listened. And that discomfort sat with me for a long time after watching the film (seven years ago to be precise).

Here's the problem: How is it possible for Samantha to experience what sounds like visceral, bodily pleasure, when she doesn't have a body? I don't think she can.

Why not? Because it's impossible to experience emotion without a body.

I think there are strong arguments for why Samantha is incapable of feeling pleasure, or any emotion at all. But before I get to those, it's important to see why this is important. I hear you ask "Why the hell should I care whether an AI can experience an orgasm?"

Well, consider this. If I'm right, if AIs can't *feel* in the full sense of the word, this has important consequences for a wide array of problems, including how we should think about life after death, and the annihilation of the world by machines.

To see why, suppose for a moment that it's impossible to experience emotion without a body. This would throw a rather large spanner in religious philosophies that hold that a person survives the death of her body through the continuation of her immortal, non-physical soul. I take it that for you to remain yourself after death, you would need to experience at least some emotions. But the soul that survives death lacks a body. So that soul would experience no emotions, and therefore wouldn't be *you*.

Science fiction authors and film makers have dreamed for decades of uploading their consciousness to a virtual computer network (i.e. the cloud) after death. But since you don't have a body in the cloud, you won't emote in the cloud either. And so, whatever exists in the cloud after your physical body dies, it won't be *you* (if you haven't done so yet, watch *Transcendence*).

Finally, consider the recent fears among the cyber elite around the development of AI. Stephen Hawking, Elon Musk, and Bill Gates have all warned that the development of a full-blown AI threatens the existence of humanity. "The development of full artificial intelligence could spell the end of the human race," said Stephen Hawking.

At the root of this concern is the fear that AIs would develop goals and desires that conflict with our own, and so, formulate a plan to eliminate us. But if I'm right, if it's impossible to experience emotion without a body, then AIs cannot have 'desires' – at least they can't if they don't have bodies. AIs cannot develop sinister intentions. Sure, they might proceed to fulfill objectives that just so happen to run counter to the wellbeing of humans. But they wouldn't be the cold-blooded, sadistic machines we find in films like *Terminator*, or novels like the prequels to *Dune*.

Alright. So, the stakes are high. It's crucial to know, one way or another, whether Samantha is capable of experiencing an orgasm. The very future of humanity (and our immortal souls) depends on it. Never has performance pressure been so high. So, here are my reasons for thinking that she can't – that emotions require a body.

While I watched the "sex" scene, I couldn't help but feel that Samantha wasn't really experiencing pleasure. She wasn't really emoting. Why? Because she doesn't know *what it's like* to feel pleasure. That is, she doesn't experience the *qualia* of sexual pleasure.

Okay, you say. Hang on just a second. What are "qualia"? Well, to answer that, imagine for a moment what it's like to be a bat. That's right. Imagine what it's like to be a squeaky flying mammal that lives upside down in dark, musty caves, and sees using sonar.

How's that imagining coming along? Can you imagine what it's like to see using sonar? I can't. Thomas Nagel, the imaginative philosopher who came up with this thought experiment, couldn't. Sure, we can dissect a bat and study the parts of its brain responsible for its echolocation ability. But that won't tell us *what it feels like* to see with sonar. The only way we could know what it's like to be a bat, is to actually be a bat! In Nagel's words, you can't experience the *qualia* of being a bat unless you *are* a bat.

Now the same holds true of Samantha's orgasm. The

only way Samantha could possibly experience bodily pleasure is if Samantha had a *body*.

You can't know bat-ness without being a bat. And you can't know bodily pleasure without having a body.

In this way, emotions are very much like colour perception. Imagine Mary, a girl who grows up in a black and white, colourless room. She's never left the room, and she's never seen colour before. Now, imagine trying to explain to Mary what colour is. "What's red?" she asks. It seems no matter how well you describe the color e.g. the wavelength of red light and even if Mary becomes a super smart scientist who investigates everything there is to know about colour, Mary will never really know what it's like to see red. Not until she leaves the room, and sees a firetruck, or a strawberry, or a stop sign, for the first time.

"Wait!" you shout. "There's a problem." You might grant that *certain* emotions or sensations are impossible without a body. Orgasms and physical pain, for example, might be impossible without a body. But perhaps other, less bodily, emotions are possible. It seems like Samantha could experience fear, or desire, or loneliness. You hear it in her voice. Surely, it's possible that she feels these emotions?

I don't think so. And the reason is that my 'gut' intuition on this is that all emotions have an essential bodily component. What is fear if it doesn't involve a quickening of the heart? What is loneliness, if you don't feel an ache in your chest? What is terror without the icy fingers of shock scrabbling across the nape of your neck?

Emotion without a corresponding bodily, physiological response is not emotion at all. All that's left is a dry husk of thought. And this is why I just can't believe it. There's just no way: Samantha can't experience an orgasm. That's bad news for your immortal soul, but at least we don't have to worry about the Terminator gunning for us any time soon.

Marriage and the Impossibility of Choice

Jason Werbeloff

A nine-year-old boy stands on a railway platform – one hand in his mother's, one hand in his father's. "So Nemo, have you made up your mind? Do you want to come with me, or do you want to stay with your father?" asks his mother. He looks from his father to his mother. To his father. To his mother.

Mr. Nobody (2009) is the best film I've ever seen. And I don't say this lightly. The movie deals with dozens of psychological and philosophical issues. It interweaves questions around freedom, death, love, time, incest, string theory, and memory, to such an extent that the film becomes a love letter to the universe, and a tribute to the capacity of the human imagination.

Above all, *Mr. Nobody* is a film about the impossibility of choice. How does Nemo choose which parent to spend his life with? How do we, any of us, make the impossibly difficult decisions we inevitably face? How do we decide which partner to marry? Whether to have children? Which career path to pursue? Whether to emigrate?

Thankfully philosophers, and *Mr. Nobody,* have much to say about these problems. By the end of this (spoiler free) section , you may have a fresh perspective on how to make big choices.

Two weeks ago, I proposed to my partner. I've made many quips in the past about Mrs. Werbeloff on my blog, both because Mrs. Werbeloff isn't female, and because we're not married. Little did I know at the time how prescient this reference was. For quite some time before proposing, I'd grappled with the decision about whether or not to get married. Because in addition to all the relational difficulties associated with getting married (and the legal and social quagmire of gay marriage), there was one massive philosophical problem that had plagued me for months:

It's impossible to get married.

Yup. I hear you. Of course it's *possible* to get married. The question isn't whether you *can* get married. It's whether you *should*?

But here's where things get interesting. Consider for a moment what's involved in getting married. Sure, legal contracts are signed. And (hopefully) lots of smiles and congratulations get passed around (or *mazeltovs*, in the case of my family). But above all, marriage is a *promise*. It's a commitment that you will stay with your spouse *for the rest of your lives*.

Nemo, the nine-year-old boy on the train platform, must make a similar commitment. Does he leave with his mother on the train, or stay with his father? He knows that this choice will alter not just his relationship with his parents, but the sort of life he'll lead from then on. If he leaves with his mother, he'll grow up in the city, meet entirely different people, and fall in love with a girl he would never meet if he continued to live with his father. Standing on that platform, which parent does he choose? Which life does he choose?

At this point, the movie splits.

We follow the life of Nemo if he'd left with his mother. And, switching back and forth with gorgeous scene transitions, we follow, in parallel, Nemo's life if he'd stayed with his father. At every point that Nemo faces a critical decision in either of these branches, his life splits again. And then yet again. Until we follow Nemo through a plethora of unique lives.

The concept is mind-tingling. The film's execution is breathtaking. And the message is clever.

To make an impossibly uncertain decision, Nemo must first imagine, decades ahead, the possible outcomes of his choices. He must, in other words, gather more information in a situation where there is no information available. To do this, he can only construct parallel narratives, or stories, about how his life might turn out.

So far so good. The film suggests we must carefully attempt to predict the outcomes of our possible choices before we make them. But there's a more fundamental problem — a problem that won't go away even in the presence of *complete* information about what will happen if we choose a certain path. The issue is this:

When you make a long-term commitment, you choose a life on behalf of a future self who isn't you.

"What the fuck does that mean?" you ask. "A future what?"

Consider who you were five years ago. Ten years ago. Fifteen. How much of yourself today do you have in common with that fifteen-years-younger self? Probably not all that much. First off, you share almost none of your physical matter with that younger self. Over time, all of our body's cells are replaced. In addition, that younger self was psychologically very different. Fifteen years ago, I was a painfully awkward seventeen-year-old who wasn't capable of much rationality at all. In hindsight, that seventeen-year-old Jason knew a lot less than he thought he did. In fact, seventeen-year-old me and today's me are so different, I don't think we're the *same* person.

Imagine your fifteen-year-younger self making decisions on your behalf today. Imagine asking that upstart what career decisions you should make, or which partner you should marry. Hell, imagine asking them to choose what you should drink tonight. They'd probably make very different choices to the decisions you'd make today.

But when you get married today, you're making a promise that you'll not only stay with your partner while you're *this* self. You're also promising that your future selves, which will become more and more dissimilar to your current self over time, will love and cherish this partner's future selves (which will also become more and more dissimilar to the partner you marry today).

It's a mess. In fact, it's the kind of mess that's so messy, we might think it's *impossible*.

Suppose you're walking through a shopping mall with a friend. You point to a random stranger, and say to your friend, "I promise that he will buy you an ice cream." Your friend would probably look at you with equal parts concern and confusion. "But you can't make that promise for him. You don't even know him."

And that's the problem. Seventeen-year-old Jason

doesn't know me. He isn't me. He can't make promises on my behalf, just as you can't make promises on behalf of the random stranger in the shopping mall. Suppose you walked up to this stranger, and informed him that he now owes your friend an ice cream. He'd deny that *he* had ever made the promise. And if you told him you had made the promise on his behalf, he'd probably tell you where to shove it. The problem is this:

It's impossible to make a promise on behalf of someone else. And with enough time, your future self is *not you*.

So it's *impossible* to make a long-term commitment, or promise, of any sort at all.

Another way of stating the problem is this. Over the years, our *qualities* change – the features of our bodies and minds. But with enough qualitative change, there is also a *numerical* change. The me of today and the me of fifteen years ago are so qualitatively different, we no longer count as a single individual. We're now two people. We're *numerically distinct*. And you can't make a commitment, or promise, on behalf of a numerically distinct person.

"Hold on!" you shout. "This is crazy. We *do* make

long-term commitments. People get married. They choose career paths. They emigrate. They *do make these decisions*. Long-term commitments. So how is it possible that they're making these commitments if such commitment is logically impossible? What's going on in those cases?"

Think for a moment what life is actually like if I'm right that you are a numerically distinct person from your younger self. Your entire life is a series of experiences *not of your choosing*.

You're repeatedly saddled with situations that a prior version of you (who isn't you) chose on your behalf, and you do the best you can with the situation you've got.

What a life.

But we still haven't answered our initial question. How do we decide between two options that will dramatically alter our life's trajectory, no matter which we choose? How does nine-year-old Nemo decide which parent to live with? How do I decide whether to propose to my partner?

The answer, I think, relies on the notion of an

opportunity loss. Sure, you have no right, and maybe you're not even capable, of making a choice on behalf of your future self. But *not making that choice is also a choice*. If I marry my partner now, my future self is saddled with a promise he didn't make. But if I *don't* marry my partner today, my future self is deprived of a union he may yet want. He's deprived of an opportunity I could have given him.

So you do something impossible. Something crazy. You cobble together the little information you can, and with eyes mostly shut ... you point to a random future version of yourself who isn't you, and promise the world on his behalf. You take the plunge. And like future Nemo, you do it with a smile.

The Taste of Gore

Jason Werbeloff

One day, something inside me changed.

Those of you who've read my fiction know that I often employ gore in my stories. Characters are regularly decapitated, eaten, or thrown off buildings. And my novel, _Defragmenting Daniel: The Organ Scrubber_, is a gore fest. I've never seen a problem with treating my characters in this way. A movie I saw a few years ago, however, has made me think twice.

One night, I watched *Hardcore Henry* (2015).

Hardcore Henry is an adrenaline-fueled bloodbath about a soldier who is brought back to life with a mash of human and cybernetic parts. But before Henry has a chance to enjoy his new life, an evil scientist hunts Henry down to obtain his technology. The movie is an unrelenting catalogue of the ways Henry annihilates the mercenaries pursuing him (for the record, there are no spoilers in this section, so it won't diminish your experience if you intend to watch the movie).

To get a disturbingly visceral sense of the gore in *Hardcore Henry*, I recommend that you watch the movie's opening credits.

Yup. Hectic. I found myself cringing in my seat. And the rest of the film is no softer. As I watched on, I got to thinking: is showing this level of gore tasteful?

There are two popular views on gore in films and literature. Some feel that it's awful, unnecessary, boring, and (at its worst) immoral garbage – call these the Conservatives. On the other hand, Gore Lovers feel quite the opposite – it's fun, often witty, and entertaining.

While I watched *Hardcore Henry*, I vacillated quite uncomfortably between these two positions. I'm not sure this was the intention of the director – I have a feeling Ilya Naishuller belongs firmly to the Gore Lovers group. And I thought I did too. But while I watched knives pierce throats in slow motion, with every serration of the blade captured in high definition as it shreds the flesh of its victim, something didn't sit quite right with me.

By the time I'd arrived home, I was in two minds about the Philosophy of Gore. I'm going to take a look at arguments for both the Conservative and Gore Loving positions, and argue that neither position is defensible. But what is particularly troubling is that I don't think the *Sometimes* position works either.

One of the most obvious arguments offered by Conservatives is that the use of gore in fiction disrespects, or degrades, the human body. "How can you *enjoy* watching this?" they ask. Living, breathing persons inhabit human bodies. Each is a distinct individual with feelings, a family, and a history all their own. Slashing their bodies for entertainment is infantile, unnecessary, and perhaps, immoral. It shows no respect for the individual's dignity, and indeed, for the dignity of human bodies in general.

This argument, however, is problematic. For one, we think that degrading or ignoring the needs of human bodies is, at least some of the time, a good thing. Almost all religions include traditions that consciously subvert the needs of the body in favour of the mind, or soul. Buddhist monks renounce pleasures of the flesh to achieve enlightenment. Historically, Catholics used self-flagellation as a tool for purification of the soul. And Jews fast on Yom Kippur to atone for their sins.

In addition, it seems like some movies and films use gore in a way that's bizarrely aesthetically pleasing. In some of the best films ever made – *The Fly, Re-Animator,* and *Kill Bill* – you can't help but gawp with equal parts admiration and horror at just how much blood is used, and how (for want of a better word) beautiful the result is. In *Kill Bill I*, over 41 people die, and 450 gallons of blood were spilled in *Kill Bill* volumes I and II. And it's glorious. The bloodbath is delicious, and incredibly satisfying to watch. But most importantly, by the end of the film you can't help but feel that the human body has taken on new meaning.

In at least some gore movies, the body becomes a

temple. A place of worship for something chilling. Something awesome.

Alright, so the argument from the dignity of the body won't cut it. But the Conservative has a second argument up her sleeve. Some Conservatives argue that gory films glorify some of the worst kinds of trauma. I was driving on the highway once, and watched the car in front of me clip the back wheel of a garbage truck. Three men sitting on the back were flung off the top of the vehicle as it flipped twice. One of the men landed underneath the truck. One landed beside my car. Before I could do anything, he'd bled to death in front of me, his blood boiling on the tar.

A decade later, I still feel a chill pass through me when I drive past that spot. Is it right, is it good art, is it necessary, to use the fragility of the body for entertainment purposes, given the seriousness of the trauma associated with violent bodily harm? People died in that crash. And many others have witnessed far worse acts of bodily gore in real life than I have. When they watch a gory movie, they may be triggered into remembering the ghastliness of those events. It seems that filmmakers and writers who produce gory entertainment are glorifying something that for some is a vicious trauma.

This argument has gained traction recently in liberal arts college campuses in the US and the UK. Books and films that might be found disturbing to victims (or survivors) of trauma are either removed from the syllabi, or are included as optional reads with "trigger warnings" inserted. "If you've been a victim of x trauma, you might find this difficult to read."

The problem, however, with trigger warnings is that their inclusion shows a fundamental misunderstanding of the responsibility of persons for their emotions. My emotions occur inside me, and so, my emotions are my responsibility. Taking the position that fiction producers should create trigger warnings to protect my emotions implies that others are responsible for my emotions. And this seems fundamentally mistaken to me.

Sure, others can influence my emotions, and in some cases can force me to feel certain feelings. A victim of brainwashing or rape might be forced to feel a certain way, but this is only because in these situations the victim is unable to remove herself from the influence of the perpetrator. In these limited cases, the perpetrator does seem responsible for the emotions felt by the victim. But in the case of a film or book, the viewer or reader is able to stop watching or reading at any time. The reader isn't victim to the book. Indeed, the reader needn't have picked up the book to begin with. There is no coercion on the part of the director or writer.

I've argued that the arguments for the Conservative position are unconvincing. Does that mean that we have a green light for including as much gore as we like in films and books? Are the Gore Lovers correct?

No, I don't think so. And here's why.

Think for a moment about gory snuff films (snuff films are recordings of actual murders of actual people). My intuition is that enjoying these sorts of films is deeply problematic. It would be difficult to construct an argument for the value of these sorts of movies, except maybe to solve a crime. But so far as entertainment goes, I think most people would agree that snuff films are bad morally and aesthetically.

So where does this leave us? Well, it seems like the only position we can take now is that including gore in fiction is tasteful *sometimes*, but not always. This position, however, raises a difficult question:

How do we know exactly when gore is appropriate? The gore in *The Fly* (1986), *Re-Animator* (1985), and *Kill Bill* (2003-2004) seems tasteful to me. But others might disagree. What principle can we provide for when gore is appropriate, and when it isn't?

This requires a lot more discussion, and we don't have space to do that here. But this is one possibility: we might think that gore is tasteful when it's used by writers or directors as a means to a greater end. Gore in *Schindler's List*, for example, is used to highlight the atrocities of the Nazi regime. On this position, using gore purely for gore's sake is tasteless. But tasteful, provided it serves a greater purpose.

The problem with this position is that it's overly restrictive. Almost no gory movies today use gore in such a serious way. Only movies intent on social commentary would be able to include gore and be deemed tasteful. But must every movie include social commentary? Watch the phenomenal Bridge Scene from *Deadpool*. Some viewers think that it's in bad taste. I don't. But it involves gore for gore's sake.

So, where do we stand now? The Conservative position is too strong. The Gore Lovers position is too weak to exclude snuff films. And the Sometimes position is vague. Maybe there is no fact of the matter about what is tasteful? Maybe taste, after all, is purely in the mouth of the consumer.

About the Authors

JASON WERBELOFF is a science fiction author with a PhD in philosophy. He has published over a dozen novels, and co-hosts the *Brain in a Vat* philosophy YouTube channel with Mark Oppenheimer.

HELEN SARAH ROBERTSON completed her doctorate in philosophy at University College London. She lectures at the University of the Witwatersrand.

MARK OPPENHEIMER studied philosophy at the University of Cape Town. He is a practicing advocate at the Johannesburg Bar, and has appeared in the Supreme Court of Appeal and the Constitutional Court.

Printed in Great Britain
by Amazon